# FOLLOWING JESUS

## *in the Details of Life*

*A Guide for 10 Minute
Daily Conversations with Our Lord*

# FOLLOWING JESUS

## *in the Details of Life*

## *Chris J. Fenner*

TATE PUBLISHING
AND ENTERPRISES, LLC

Published by Tate Publishing & Enterprises, LLC
127 E. Trade Center Terrace | Mustang, Oklahoma 73064 USA
1.888.361.9473 | www.tatepublishing.com

Tate Publishing is committed to excellence in the publishing industry. The company reflects the philosophy established by the founders, based on Psalm 68:11,
*"The LORD gave the word and great was the company of those who published it."*

Book design copyright © 2012 by Tate Publishing, LLC. All rights reserved.
*Cover design by Kristen Verser*
*Interior design by Christina Hicks*

Published in the United States of America

ISBN: 978-1-61862-344-7
1. Religion / Christian Life / Devotional
2. Religion / Christian Life / Personal Growth
12.02.21

# *Acknowledgments*

Many people were part of my coming to know the Lord and my learning to follow Jesus in the details of life—the following are those who have been particularly precious to me.

My mother, Vera May Blay, who was a living example of "following Jesus in the details of life."

My friend and coworker Sheryl Garret, who witnessed to me in a silent yet profound way as he lived a life of "following Jesus in the details of life," even as his wife suffered and died through a long battle with cancer.

The godly men in Santa Barbara, California, who encouraged me during the two-year sabbatical from my career in the oil industry as I sought the Lord and His will for my life—especially Al Phau, who God used in a powerful way to direct me back to work.

Steve Wetch, Luiz Bensimon, Max Lewis, Janet Pool, Wendy Landry, Susan Martin, and Cassandra Massee, who joined with me in prayer, fellowship, and Bible Study at Imodco Inc. in Agoura Hills, California.

Kevin McCaffery, Bill Kramer, Doug Milliken, Scott Bailey, Ken Ellsworth, Tim Cleary—longtime members of a men's small group in Westlake Village, California—now lifetime friends.

Pastor Gordy Duncan, Tori Yamada, Len Sunukian, Willett Tuitele, Dan Morgan, Gail Irwin, Chris Steffen—faithful pray-ers for God's glory.

Chris Hartman, Matt Svoboda, John Gommel, Danny Ayala, Martin Fuentes, and the other men and women at the SBM companies in Houston, who regularly met together for Bible study, fellowship, and prayer.

Pastor Steve Bass, Travis Brunner, Charlie Crawford, Edward Sneider, Mike Kelly, Ron Gere, Martin Fuentes—men who helped me refine this study guide by their participation in Saturday morning study groups.

Sharon Tice and Tori Yamada—wonderful and faithful prayer partners and prayer warriors, who I can always turn to for intercessory prayer.

Most of all—in all things and through all things—my wife, Diana.

Also I have been greatly blessed to work with a wonderful team at Tate Publishing that included: Joey Garrett, Rachael Sweeden, Lauren Downen, Katja Nichols, Amanda Soderberg, Thomas Beard, Kristen Verser, and Christina Hicks.

# Reaction From Participants

Here are some reactions from participants in the *Following Jesus in the Details of Life* study.

"God spoke to me through His Word.  Here was a bible study that drew me in first thing daily.  I loved writing how God spoke to me and sharing with my group on Saturday mornings.  Thanks, Chris!"

—Charlie Crawford

"*Following Jesus in the Details of Life* is unique in that it allows the participant to be absorbed in particular scriptures pertaining to the topic of the week.  The reflection questions and challenges give great insight into the various aspects of knowing, abiding and achieving victory in Jesus.  This study involved me in an opportunity to deepen my faith journey as I rediscovered the unique blessings of the Christian life.  The experience was personal and intimate drawing me closer to the Savior."

—Jennifer Stuckey

"God spoke to me through the scriptures in *Following Jesus in the Details of Life* and this helped me to come to know myself and to change the things God wanted me to change so that I joyfully and willingly obey Him."

—Diana Fenner

"*Following Jesus in the Details of Life* made me focus on what was most important in my life—my faith in God—during a time when my life had many competing priorities.  The selected Bible verses and associated questions made me dig deep to uncover my beliefs. This produced rich discussions in the weekly group meetings that lead to application of those beliefs to my life situation. How powerful and encouraging this was!"

—Charlie Matcek

"If I have a chance to go through this study again, I most certainly will do so."

—Betty Schwarz

"The more I study this book the more God becomes real in my life and gives my spirit strength; my faith grows and my love for others expands. My love for my wife has been renewed through this study and I am feeling something special for her like when we first met."

—Martin Fuentes

"I have gained tremendous spiritual benefit from studying *Following Jesus in the Details of Life*. The sections contain valuable Biblical information that I will always use."

—John Songu

# Table of Contents



## Part I: Knowing Him



## Part II: Abide in Him



## Part III: His Victory

# *Preface*

I came to know our Lord in midlife and spent two years away from my career in the oil industry seeking to find a different path of life that I thought the Lord was leading me to. However, at the end of these two years, it became clear that I was to return to my previous type of work, but now in His service.

As I started this new, and renewed, phase of life, the question came to my mind: "Okay, I am now a Christian. How am I supposed to behave?" In this I sought the Lord, and over a three-month period, the writing for "Knowing Him" (see the opening page of Part 1) came to me, and this became an outline guide for my daily thoughts and perspective.

Over the next five years, I was led by the Lord to develop this single writing into a study guide that I could use with other men to learn how to live for the Lord in all of life, including the workplace. It was through these meetings with several different groups of men over the next fifteen years that *Following Jesus in the Details of Life* emerged in its final form.

The focus of this guide is God's Word, and through the meditation on twenty-six topics—by daily reading of short passages of the Bible—God will speak to your heart and reveal His presence to you in living and active ways.

—Chris Fenner,
June 2011

# How To Use This Study Guide

Imagine that your favorite recent President of the United States asked you to spend ten minutes with him every day, at which time he would give you his undivided attention, listen attentively to you, and impart his wisdom to you on topics that were nearest and dearest to your heart. For most people, such a privilege would be a huge honor and joy that they would look forward to with great anticipation every day.

This is just a small illustration of how our daily devotional time with our Lord should be, but instead of meeting with the President of the United States we are meeting with the King of kings, the Lord of lords, the Lord God Almighty. He, even more so, gives us His undivided attention and imparts His wisdom to us for that day that is infinitely beyond the wisdom of any man. Shame on us that we are not excited about each moment in His presence as we often prefer to forgo time with the Creator and Sustainer of all things to do something that appears to be a priority to us, but has no lasting importance!

●

This study guide is a tool to help you build the wonderful discipline of spending time with our Lord in a very meaningful way as described above. The daily Bible readings take no more than five minutes to read, so even if you are hard pressed for time the devotional of Bible reading and prayer can be completed in ten minutes. And what a blessed ten minutes this will be—ten minutes that will change your life!

●

There is benefit in using this as a personal study guide; however, the benefit is greatly enhanced with weekly small group meetings (groups of two to no more than six people are recommended) where the discussion of how the Lord has 'spoken' through His Word on the topic for the week is reinforced.

●

Both men's groups and women's groups have used the study guide with equal effectiveness. However, it is not recommended for mixed groups since the guide leads to the heart of our sinful natures and these topics can be more openly and effectively discussed in same-sex groups.

My prayer is that this guide will help you draw closer to God in every detail of life.

## The Voice of the Lord

In this study guide you will see the phrase: 'How did the Lord speak to you today?' with each daily Bible reading and you may wonder what this means. The key is to remember that our Lord wants to have a conversation with you and His 'voice' may come to you in many different ways and at unexpected times.

As I struggled with this same question some years ago I wrote the following prose, delighting in the many ways the Lord speaks to us, and this may help you to understand the diverse ways that our Lord speaks to His children.

YOUR VOICE

I delight, O Lord, in your voice!

You speak to us through the scriptures from Genesis to Malachi, from Matthew to Revelation, that we may know You more, that we may love You more (see Psalm 119:105).

You speak to us through Your Spirit, made possible by Jesus dying for our sins, that we may know You more, that we may love You more (see John 7:38).

You speak to us through Your creation: the heavens, even the highest heavens, and the earth with all its beauty, that we may know You more, that we may love You more (see Isaiah 6:3b).

You speak to us in answer to our prayers, that we may know You more, that we may love You more (see 1 John 5:14).

You speak to us through Your faithful servants, both those with us and the legacies of those with You, that we may know You more, that we may love You more (see Ephesians 4:11).

You speak to us through fellowship with other believers in many diverse and surprising ways, that we may know You more, that we may love You more (see Hebrews 10:24).

You speak to us through the details of life and the wonderful 'coincidences' that can only come from You, that we may know You more, that we may love You more (see 2 Corinthians 9:8).

You speak to us through the events of each day: the joys, the sorrows; the victories, the defeats, that we may know You more, that we may love You more (see Romans 8:28).

You speak to us, at times, through visions and dreams to fulfill Your purposes, and that we may know You more, that we may love You more (see Acts 2:17b).

I delight, O Lord, in your voice!

Yes, even to hear You speak (see 1 Samuel 3:9b).

## *How To Be A Weekly Meeting Facilitator*

To be the facilitator for weekly meetings requires only two attributes: to be a model of daily meeting with our Lord in the assigned scriptures and in prayer; and to be willing to share your joys and despairs, and your victories and defeats on the pilgrimage of *Following Jesus in the Details of Life*.

•

The recommended format of the weekly meetings is:

- opening prayer to usher in the Holy Spirit,

- discussion on how the Lord has 'spoken' to each person in the group through the daily Bible readings, prayer and living life (this should take up most of the time),

- reading the opening section for the introduction and quotation for the next week,

- discussion on the Reflection Question,

- reading the Challenge and Memory Verse,

- closing prayer.

One hour is typically needed for the weekly meeting.

# *Week 1: Introduction*

Do all things work together in your life so that you are able to fulfill your responsibilities and the desires of your heart without worry or distress?

> And we know that in all things God works for the good of those who love him, who have been called according to his purpose.
>
> Romans 8:28

Are the fruit of the Spirit manifest in your life such that they are evident to other people?

> But the fruit of the Spirit is love, joy, peace, patience, kindness, goodness, faithfulness, gentleness and self-control.
>
> Galatians 5:22-23a

Do you walk in the fullness of Christ with His gifts manifest in your life through the grace of God?

> But to each one of us grace has been given as Christ apportioned it.
>
> Ephesians 4:7

Do you know our Savior so intimately that His purpose and your purpose in life are one?

> I have made you known to them, and will continue to make you known in order that the love you have for me may be in them and that I myself may be in them. [Jesus' prayer for all believers.]
>
> John 17:26

Is your life a continual witness to the lost and to the saved?

> For we are to God the aroma of Christ among those who are being saved and those who are perishing.
>
> 2 Corinthians 2:15

The gospel of Jesus Christ promises an answer of, "Yes!" to these questions. Yet we are so often mired in the ways of the world, saved yet lost to many of the promises of our Savior.

After His resurrection, Jesus gave His disciples what we call today the Great Commission: "Therefore go and make disciples…" (Matthew 28:19a). He said this because He knew, for God's will to be done in our lives and for the fullness of the good news to be manifest in our lives, we must move beyond knowing Him merely as our Savior. He knew that we would need to be His true followers—His disciples.

Consequently, to get out of the mire of this world, we must become true disciples of Jesus Christ. And to become true disciples, we must allow Jesus to lead us from a life that follows the ways of the world to a life where the Spirit of God fills us so that we may fulfill His purpose for us. This is the promise of Jesus when he tells us, "If you love me, you will obey what I command. And I will ask the Father, and he will give you another Counselor to be with you forever—the Spirit of truth …" (John 14:15-17a).

But how can this become a meaningful reality in our lives?

Five books of the Bible, Exodus through Joshua, are devoted to the story of the Israelites' journey out of captivity into the Promised Land. This story contains important parallels for us today as we also make a journey from being captive to the ways of the world to the "promised land" of a life filled with the presence of Jesus.

Some key points of the story of the Israelites' journey are as follows:

- They were God's chosen people while they were still in captivity in Egypt.

- God led them to the Promised Land by the way of the desert to test their hearts.

- After the initial excitement of leaving captivity, they quickly yearned for their old way of life.

- When it came time to enter the Promised Land, many were afraid, and they turned aside only to wander in the desert.

- As they trusted wholeheartedly in God, so the time came to enter the Promised Land, but this involved many battles.

- Finally, God's promise of living in a land filled with 'milk and honey' was fulfilled.

Once we accept Jesus Christ, we too are God's chosen people, but like the Israelites, we are still in captivity—captive to the ways of the world (1 Peter 2:9). And we are called out of this "captivity" to follow Jesus to the "promised land" of a life filled with His presence and marked by the fruit of the Spirit (Galatians 5:22-23). The road to this "promised land," however, also passes through a desert where God tests our hearts, and it is in this suffering that we break free from our old natures and learn to abide in Him.

Also the way into the "promised land" of a Spirit-filled life is not easy, but it is a fight—a fight that only Jesus can win. The enemy is the great deceiver who wants us to stay captive to the ways of the world. But thanks be to God! He gives us the victory through our Lord Jesus Christ (1 Corinthians 15:57).

This then is the foundation of *Following Jesus in the Details of Life*: to abide in the Lord, to know the indwelling Holy Spirit, to find peace and joy, and to be a light in a world of darkness.

Each person's journey to this "promised land" is different, but the promise of the abundant life where the "streams of living water will flow from within" is the same (John 7:38).

The first part of *Following Jesus in the Details of Life* is "Knowing Him," which covers the basic principles of living a Christian life.

The second part is the journey across the desert where God tests our hearts as we learn to "Abide In Him."

Finally, "His Victory" covers the battle to enter the "promised land" where Jesus gains full control of our lives so that we can know His marvelous blessings: the fruit of the Spirit, the gifts of the Spirit that have been apportioned to us, the fullness of God's grace, and a desire to serve only Him.

## Challenge for This Week

It is important to establish a daily routine for Bible reading and prayer; therefore, this is the main challenge for the first week. Read the assigned daily Bible passage included in this study guide accompanied by a time of prayer. And remember, you are entering into the presence of our heavenly Father, the Lord God Almighty, for a one-on-one conversation with Him every day! He gives you His time and is waiting for you. How can we not make this a priority and a joyful privilege?

## Readings for Week 1: Introduction

### Day 1-3: The Israelites' Journey

Day 1 (__/__/__) - Exodus 3:1-10 (A chosen people)

Key verse: *"So I have come down to rescue [my people] from the hand of the Egyptians and to bring them up out of that land into a good and spacious land, a land flowing with milk and honey..."* (v. 8a).

How did the Lord speak to you today and how did you respond?

_______________________________________________

_______________________________________________

_______________________________________________

_______________________________________________

Day 2 (__/__/__) - Exodus 13:17-22 (Led by the Spirit)

Key verse: *By day the LORD went ahead of them in a pillar of cloud to guide them on their way and by night in a pillar of fire to give them light, so that they could travel by day or night* (v. 21).

How did the Lord speak to you today and how did you respond?

_______________________________________________

_______________________________________________

_______________________________________________

_______________________________________________

Day 3 ( __/__/__) - Joshua 23:1-16 (To the Promised Land)

Key verse: *"You know with all your heart and soul that not one of all the good promises the LORD your God gave you has failed. Every promise has been fulfilled;..."* (v. 14b).

How did the Lord speak to you today and how did you respond?

_______________________________________________

_______________________________________________

_______________________________________________

_______________________________________________

## Day 4-6 Our Journey

Day 4 (__/__/__) - 1 Peter 2:4-12 (A chosen people)

Key verse: *But you are a chosen people, a royal priesthood, a holy nation, a people belonging to God, that you may declare the praises of him who called you out of darkness into his wonderful light* (v. 9).

How did the Lord speak to you today and how did you respond?

_______________________________________________________________________

_______________________________________________________________________

_______________________________________________________________________

_______________________________________________________________________

Day 5 (__/__/__) - John 16:5-16 (Led by the Spirit)

Key verse: *"But when he, the Spirit of truth, comes, he will guide you into all truth."* (v.13a).

How did the Lord speak to you today and how did you respond?

_______________________________________________________________________

_______________________________________________________________________

_______________________________________________________________________

_______________________________________________________________________

Day 6 (__/__/__) - Galatians 5:16-26 (To the "promised land")

Key verse: *But the fruit of the Spirit is love, joy, peace, patience, kindness, goodness, faithfulness, gentleness, and self-control* (vv. 22-23a).

How did the Lord speak to you today and how did you respond?

_______________________________________________________________________

_______________________________________________________________________

_______________________________________________________________________

_______________________________________________________________________

# Part I: Knowing Him

**May I** have faith to know You are always present to guide me.

**May I** have hope to know that my trust in You will not be disappointed.

**May I** have love toward all people I meet this day.


**May I** remember that it is not for me to direct my own steps, but to follow Your way.

**May I** remember that it is not for me to seek power over others, but to serve others.

**May I** remember that it is not for me to worry about tomorrow, but to gladly do Your will this day.


**May I** know the peace and confidence that comes from following Your way.

**May I** know the joy that springs from this peace as I see You move in the lives of those who love You.

**May I** know that all of this is possible as I pray and give praise in all things.


Amen.

This prayer is to remind us of the principles of Christian living; consequently, each verse is a signpost to a greater truth in God's Word.

# *Week 2: Faith*

## *May I have faith to know You are always present to guide me.*

The meaning of faith has become diluted in our society as there has been a movement away from the true God. However, the meaning of Christian faith is unchanging; that is to say, "Love the Lord your God with all your heart and with all your soul and with all your mind" (Matthew 22:37b). It is by loving the Lord in the fullness of the Great Commandment that His Presence, the Holy Spirit, guides us in all truth.

> There is a faith of insight, a faith of desire, a faith of trust in the truth of the word, and a faith of personal acceptance. There is a faith of love that embraces, a faith of will that holds fast, and a faith of sacrifice that gives up everything, and a faith of despair that abandons all hope in self, and a faith of rest that waits on God alone. This is all included in the faith of a true heart, the fullness of faith, in which the whole being surrenders and lets go all, and yields itself to God to do His work. In fullness of faith let us draw near.
>
> —*Andrew Murray* [1]

I have found that our walk with the Lord is more one of deletion than addition. The Lord does not want to add greater burdens to our lives as we seek and strive to do His work; rather He wants to simplify our lives so that we release everything related to our old, worldly natures and trust only in Him. This simplicity is expressed beautifully in Genesis 5:24 where the writer tells us, "Enoch walked with God"; and the same need for this simple walk with God came to me as I struggled to live the life I saw that God had called me to live.

THE WIND OF THE SPIRIT

The ship *My Lord God Almighty* is ready, but the anchor is still set and the sails are still furled—even though the fair wind of the Spirit is blowing—for I am still in the waters of struggling faith trying to get to the ship.

The ship *My Lord God Almighty* is ready, but the anchor is still set and the sails are still furled—even though the fair wind of the Spirit is blowing—for I am still in the waters of clinging faith holding onto the side of the ship.

The ship *My Lord God Almighty* is ready with the anchor raised and the sails unfurled, and the fair wind of the Spirit is blowing. Now resting faith has brought me into the ship ready to embark on the journey of life for His glory.

## *Reflections and Questions*

Review the author's experience on page 21 and think about situations where your faith is strong and where your faith is still fragile?

## *Challenge for This Week*

This week pray that God may reveal to you the things that you are withholding from Him; that is to say, where you have struggling faith or clinging faith.

---

## *Memory Verse*

Love the Lord your God with all your heart and with all your soul and with all your mind.

Matthew 22:37b

---

## *Readings for Week 2: Faith*

Day 1 (__/__/__) - Genesis 22:1-14

Key verse: *So Abraham called that place The Lord Will Provide. And to this day it is said, "On the mountain of the Lord it will be provided."* (v. 14).

How did the Lord speak to you today and how did you respond?

____________________________________________________

____________________________________________________

____________________________________________________

____________________________________________________

Day 2 (__/__/__) - Matthew 14:22-36

Key verse: *Immediately Jesus reached out his hand and caught him. "You of little faith," he said, "why did you doubt?"* (v. 31).

How did the Lord speak to you today and how did you respond?

____________________________________________________

____________________________________________________

____________________________________________________

____________________________________________________

Day 3 (__/__/__) - John 14:1-14
Key verse: *"I tell you the truth, anyone who has faith in me will do what I have been doing. He will do even greater things than these, because I am going to the Father"* (v. 12).

How did the Lord speak to you today and how did you respond?

________________________________________

________________________________________

________________________________________

________________________________________

Day 4 (__/__/__) - Romans 1:8-17
Key verse: *For in the gospel a righteousness from God is revealed, a righteousness that is by faith from first to last, just as it is written: "The righteous will live by faith"* (v. 17).

How did the Lord speak to you today and how did you respond?

________________________________________

________________________________________

________________________________________

________________________________________

Day 5 (__/__/__) - 2 Corinthians 5:1-10
Key verse: *We live by faith, not by sight* (v. 7).

How did the Lord speak to you today and how did you respond?

________________________________________

________________________________________

________________________________________

________________________________________

Day 6 (__/__/__) - Hebrews 11:1-13
Key verse: *Now faith is being sure of what we hope for and certain of what we do not see* (v. 1).

How did the Lord speak to you today and how did you respond?

________________________________________

________________________________________

________________________________________

________________________________________

# Week 3: Hope

*May I have hope to know that my trust in You will not be disappointed.*

Many people are frustrated because either they cannot find any true sense of hope and purpose in their lives, or they cannot fulfill the purpose that they have found. Moreover, if we trust only in our own efforts, this frustration will continue, but the Lord promises fulfillment when He tells us that, "Those who hope in me will not be disappointed" (Isaiah 49:23b).

> Thus, when a person is newly born of the Spirit, his grasp of God's purpose for him is usually very limited and his experience is limited in proportion. But as the Holy Spirit enlightens the eyes of his heart, vistas begin to open up before him of which at first he had scarcely even dreamed. He begins to see and know the hope of God's calling, the riches of God's inheritance and the greatness of God's power.
>
> —*John R. W. Stott* [2]

The Lord made Abraham wait for twenty-five years for the promised son to be born. The Lord allowed Joseph to wallow in a prison for over a decade before the time was right for him to become second only to Pharaoh in Egypt. Moses fled to the desolate parts of Midian when his attempt to do God's will failed, and then the Lord left him there for forty years. Why the delay in using these great men of the Bible? So that they would learn to rely only on Him and that their only hope was in Him. And so it is today. The Lord cannot use us until we shed any hope in ourselves.

IN THIS I CAN REJOICE

In this I can rejoice!
I have hope in the Lord for today. He will guide me and guard me through the difficulties.

In this I can rejoice!
I have hope in the Lord for tomorrow. He will fulfill His purpose for me.

In this I can rejoice!
I have hope in the Lord for eternity. He will lead me home to the place He has prepared.

In this I can rejoice!

## Reflections and Questions

What are your goals in life, and what provides you with hope and a sense of purpose?
What part do you think God has in bringing hope and a sense of purpose?

## Challenge for This Week

This week pray for a deeper understanding of how your relationship with Jesus Christ is related to your purpose in life.

---

### *Memory Verse*

"For I know the plans I have for you," declares the Lord, "plans to prosper you and not to harm you, plans to give you hope and a future."

Jeremiah 29:11

---

## *Readings for Week 3: Hope*

Day 1 (__/__/__) - Psalm 62:1-8

Key verse: *Find rest, O my soul, in God alone; my hope comes from him* (v. 5).

How did the Lord speak to you today and how did you respond?

_______________________________________________

_______________________________________________

_______________________________________________

_______________________________________________

Day 2 (__/__/__) - Proverbs 16:3, 19:21, 20:24, 23:17 and 18

Key verse: *Many are the plans in a man's heart, but it is the Lord's purpose that prevails* (Proverbs 19:21).

How did the Lord speak to you today and how did you respond?

_______________________________________________

_______________________________________________

_______________________________________________

_______________________________________________

Day 3 (__/__/__) - Jeremiah 29:4-14

Key verse: *"For I know the plans I have for you," declares the Lord, "plans to prosper you and not to harm you, plans to give you hope and a future."* (v. 11).

How did the Lord speak to you today and how did you respond?

_______________________________________________

_______________________________________________

_______________________________________________

_______________________________________________

Day 4 (__/__/__) - Hebrews 6:13-20
    Key verse: *We have this hope as an anchor for the soul, firm and secure* (v. 19a).

How did the Lord speak to you today and how did you respond?

___________________________________________________________________________

___________________________________________________________________________

___________________________________________________________________________

___________________________________________________________________________

Day 5 (__/__/__) - Hebrews 10:19-25
    Key verse: *Let us hold unswervingly to the hope we profess, for he who promised is faithful* (v. 23).

How did the Lord speak to you today and how did you respond?

___________________________________________________________________________

___________________________________________________________________________

___________________________________________________________________________

___________________________________________________________________________

Day 6 (__/__/__) - 1 Peter 1:13-21
    Key verse: *Therefore, prepare your minds for action; be self-controlled; set your hope fully on the grace to be given you when Jesus Christ is revealed* (v. 13).

How did the Lord speak to you today and how did you respond?

___________________________________________________________________________

___________________________________________________________________________

___________________________________________________________________________

___________________________________________________________________________

# *Week 4: Love*

## *May I have love toward all people I meet this day.*

In 1 Corinthians 13, Paul shows us "the most excellent way"—the way of love—which is as applicable today as it was to the Corinthians almost two thousand years ago.

Starting at the fourth verse of this chapter, Paul defines the meaning of love:

> Love is patient, love is kind. It does not envy, it does not boast, it is not proud. It is not rude, it is not self-seeking, it is not easily angered, it keeps no record of wrongs. Love does not delight in evil but rejoices with the truth. It always protects, always trusts, always hopes, always perseveres.
>
> 1 Corinthians 13:4-7

> So for all of us, it doesn't matter what we are doing or where we are as long as we remember that we belong to him, that we are his, that we are in love with him. The means he gives us, whether we are working for the rich or we are working for the poor, whether we are working with high-class people or low-class people, it makes no difference; but how much love we are putting into the work we do is what matters.
>
> *Mother Teresa* [3]

It is often when we stumble and fall that we learn the most. This has certainly been true for me, and in one of these times of failure, when my actions grieved a good friend and pastor who had helped me through a very difficult period in my walk with the Lord, that I realized that Jesus did not have all of my life, and the part that He did not have was still very self-centered and unloving. These words came to me and captured what I still had yet to learn.

LOVE IS …
Love is Jesus living in me.

Jesus is love and His love is alive in me if I truly love Him. Therefore if I say, "I love Jesus," yet I do not love others I deceive myself and the truth is not in me.

If I love little it is because I love Jesus little.
If I love much it is because I love Jesus much.

Love is Jesus living in me.

## *Reflections and Questions*

Rate yourself on a scale of one to ten against the definition of love described in Paul's letter to the Corinthians. Also share your self-assessment with other people in your weekly meeting to see if they can give you additional insight on how well you love others.

| | | |
|---|---|---|
| _ Patient | _ Not rude | _ Rejoice with the truth |
| _ Kind | _ Not self-seeking | _ Always protect |
| _ Do not envy | _ Not easily angered | _ Always trust |
| _ Do not boast | _ Keep no record of wrongs | _ Always hope |
| _ Not proud | _ Do not delight in evil | _ Always persevere |

## *Challenge for This Week*

In prayer, ask God for more of His presence and His love.

## *Memory Verse*

Live a life of love, just as Christ loved us and gave himself up for us as a fragrant offering and sacrifice to God.

Ephesians 5:2

## *Readings for Week 4: Love*

Day 1 (__/__/__) - Proverbs 3:1-4

Key verse: *Let love and faithfulness never leave you; bind them around your neck, write them on the tablet of your heart* (v. 3).

How did the Lord speak to you today and how did you respond?

_______________________________________________

_______________________________________________

_______________________________________________

_______________________________________________

Day 2 (__/__/__) - Mark 12:28-34

Key verse: *"The second is this: 'Love your neighbor as yourself.' There is no commandment greater than these"* (v. 31).

How did the Lord speak to you today and how did you respond?

_______________________________________________

_______________________________________________

_______________________________________________

_______________________________________________

Day 3 (__/__/__) - Luke 6:27-36
   Key verse: *"Do to others as you would have them do to you"* (v. 31).

How did the Lord speak to you today and how did you respond?

_______________________________________________________

_______________________________________________________

_______________________________________________________

_______________________________________________________


Day 4 (__/__/__) - 1 Corinthians 13:1-13
   Key verse: *And now these three remain: faith, hope and love. But the greatest of these is love* (v. 13).

How did the Lord speak to you today and how did you respond?

_______________________________________________________

_______________________________________________________

_______________________________________________________

_______________________________________________________


Day 5 (__/__/__) - Ephesians 5:1-21
   Key verse: *… and live a life of love, just as Christ loved us and gave himself up for us as a fragrant offering and sacrifice to God* (v. 2).

How did the Lord speak to you today and how did you respond?

_______________________________________________________

_______________________________________________________

_______________________________________________________

_______________________________________________________


Day 6 (__/__/__) - 1 John 4:7-21
   Key verse: *Dear friends, let us love one another, for love comes from God. Everyone who loves has been born of God and knows God* (v. 7).

How did the Lord speak to you today and how did you respond?

_______________________________________________________

_______________________________________________________

_______________________________________________________

_______________________________________________________

# Week 5: God's Way

*May I remember that it is not for me to direct my own steps,*
*but to follow Your way.*

Life can be compared to walking through a maze as each day, and often each hour of each day, we must make decisions. These may be small decisions, such as how we respond to criticism from another person, or major decisions that determine the direction of our lives, a company, or an organization. But regardless of the magnitude of the decision, the real decision is always the same: whether we will follow God's way or our own way.

Jeremiah said, "I know, O Lord, that a man's life is not his own; it is not for man to direct his steps." (Jeremiah 10:23).

> [If] we behold Jesus Christ going on before step by step, we shall not go astray. But if we worry about the dangers that beset us, if we gaze at the road instead of at him who goes before, we are already straying from the path. For he is himself the way, the narrow way and the narrow gate. He, and he alone, is our journey's end.
>
> *—Dietrich Bonhoeffer* [4]

I had followed the Lord as faithfully as I could for over twelve years when I entered a period of great trial. The vision I had from the Lord was as far as ever from being fulfilled. Some of the long term financial decisions my wife and I had made so that we could be ready to be used by the Lord appeared to have been misguided. To top it off, the transmission on both of our automobiles went out within three days of each other. As the trials deepened I got caught in a dangerous inner conflict like the motions of a crosscut saw: one day remaining faithful to my calling and the next day, full of fear, running to catch up with the ways of the world. At the height of my distress I was due to be an evangelism volunteer at a Promise Keepers event, but when I was on the field to pray for others the Lord placed on my heart to take off my EV badge and turn to another volunteer for prayer. Before this period of trial came to a close I had to realize that my Lord needed to be Lord of all regardless of my immediate circumstances.

THY WILL, O LORD

> Thy will, O Lord, not mine.
> Thy way, O Lord, not mine.
> Thy time, O Lord, not mine.
> Thy all, O Lord, not mine.

## Reflections and Questions

To what extent do you think that God is concerned about the details of our lives: at home, at work, with friends and neighbors?

## Challenge for This Week

Think about those parts of your life that still follow the world's ways and in prayer seek the Lord's guidance about how you can more fully follow His ways.

### *Memory Verse*

Then he said to them all: "If anyone would come after me, he must deny himself and take up his cross daily and follow me."

Luke 9:23

## *Readings for Week 5: God's Way*

Day 1 (__/__/__) - Deuteronomy 10:12-22

Key verse: *And now, O Israel, what does the* Lord *your God ask of you but to fear the* Lord *your God, to walk in all his ways, to love him, to serve the* Lord *your God with all your heart and with all your soul, … (v. 12).*

How did the Lord speak to you today and how did you respond?

_______________________________________________

_______________________________________________

_______________________________________________

_______________________________________________

Day 2 (__/__/__) - Isaiah 42:10-17

Key verse: *I will lead the blind by ways they have not known, along unfamiliar paths I will guide them; … (v. 16a).*

How did the Lord speak to you today and how did you respond?

_______________________________________________

_______________________________________________

_______________________________________________

_______________________________________________

Day 3 (__/__/__) - Luke 9:18-27

Key verse: *Then he said to them all: "If anyone would come after me, he must deny himself and take up his cross daily and follow me" (v. 23).*

How did the Lord speak to you today and how did you respond?

_______________________________________________

_______________________________________________

_______________________________________________

_______________________________________________

Day 4 (__/__/__) - John 12:20-36

Key verse: *"Whoever serves me must follow me; and where I am, my servant also will be. My father will honor the one who serves me"* (v. 26).

How did the Lord speak to you today and how did you respond?

_______________________________________________________________________

_______________________________________________________________________

_______________________________________________________________________

_______________________________________________________________________

Day 5 (__/__/__) - 1 Peter 2:13-25

Key verse: *To this you were called, because Christ suffered for you, leaving you an example, that you should follow in his steps* (v. 21).

How did the Lord speak to you today and how did you respond?

_______________________________________________________________________

_______________________________________________________________________

_______________________________________________________________________

_______________________________________________________________________

Day 6 (__/__/__) - 1 John 2:1-11

Key verse: *Whoever claims to live in him must walk as Jesus did* (v. 6).

How did the Lord speak to you today and how did you respond?

_______________________________________________________________________

_______________________________________________________________________

_______________________________________________________________________

_______________________________________________________________________

# Week 6: Serving Others

*May I remember that it is not for me to seek power over others,
but to serve others.*

When some of Christ's disciples selfishly sought to gain power and authority in His kingdom, He said to them, "Whoever wants to become great among you must be your servant, and whoever wants to be first must be your slave—just as the Son of Man did not come to be served, but to serve, and to give his life as a ransom for many" (Matthew 20:26-28).

As Christians we are similarly called to serve others rather than to seek power over others.

> According to faith we are in need of nothing, and have an abundance; according to love we are servants of all. By faith we receive blessings from above, from God; through love we give them out below, to our neighbor. Even as Christ in his divinity stood in need of nothing, but in his humanity served everybody who had need of him.
>
> *—Martin Luther* [5]

After I came to know the Lord in mid-life, He steered me into a job in the offshore oil industry that was very challenging, as there never seemed to be enough time and resources to do the work where I could say I was working unto the Lord. But amid these daily difficulties He showed me two things. First was the importance of faith in maintaining that vital presence of the Holy Spirit in my life so that what I was unable to do in my own strength at work, He was able to accomplish through His divine providence. Second was that He had placed me in this company for His purposes so that I could be a witness for Him by allowing His presence to be demonstrated in my life through love towards my coworkers. These two pillars of Christianity as spoken of by Jesus in the Greatest Commandment are both a constant challenge and great reward. To keep them in the forefront of my busy days I wrote this simple prose and placed it in a visible location on my office desk.

A LIFE OF FAITH AND LOVE

    A life of faith
comes from a day of faith,
comes from an hour of faith,
comes from a moment of faith.
Teach me, O Lord, to live each moment in faith.

    A life of love
comes from a day of love,
comes from an hour of love,
comes from a moment of love.
Teach me, O Lord, to live each moment with love.

Teach me, O Lord, to live each moment in faith with love.

## *Reflections and Questions*

In what ways has God given you authority over others—in your family, in your work life, in your church and social activities—and do you use this authority to serve others or to serve yourself?

## *Challenge for This Week*

God wants us to be transmitters of the love that He pours into us by acting in love towards others. As you read the Bible verses this week ask God in prayer to increase your love for Him and to increase your desire to act with love towards others.

---

## *Memory Verse*

Your attitude should be the same as that of Christ Jesus: … taking the very nature of a servant.

Philippians 2:5, 7b

---

## *Readings for Week 6: Serving Others*

Day 1 (__/__/__) - Matthew 20:20-28

Key verse: *"Instead, whoever wants to become great among you must be your servant,… just as the Son of Man did not come to be served, but to serve,"… (vv. 26b, 28a).*

How did the Lord speak to you today and how did you respond?

________________________________________________________________

________________________________________________________________

________________________________________________________________

________________________________________________________________

Day 2 (__/__/__) - Luke 22:24-27

Key verse: *"Instead, the greatest among you should be like the youngest, and the one who rules like the one who serves"* (v. 26b).

How did the Lord speak to you today and how did you respond?

________________________________________________________________

________________________________________________________________

________________________________________________________________

________________________________________________________________

Day 3 (__/__/__) - John 13:1-17
Key verse: *"I have set you an example that you should do as I have done for you"* (v. 15).

How did the Lord speak to you today and how did you respond?

_________________________________________________________________

_________________________________________________________________

_________________________________________________________________

_________________________________________________________________

Day 4 (__/__/__) - Galatians 5:1-15
Key verse: *You, my brothers, were called to be free. But do not use your freedom to indulge the sinful nature; rather, serve one another in love* (v. 13).

How did the Lord speak to you today and how did you respond?

_________________________________________________________________

_________________________________________________________________

_________________________________________________________________

_________________________________________________________________

Day 5 (__/__/__) - Philippians 2:1-11
Key verse: *Your attitude should be the same as that of Christ Jesus: … taking the very nature of a servant, …* (vv. 5, 7b).

How did the Lord speak to you today and how did you respond?

_________________________________________________________________

_________________________________________________________________

_________________________________________________________________

_________________________________________________________________

Day 6 (__/__/__) - 1 Peter 4:7-11
Key verse: *Each one should use whatever gift he has received to serve others, faithfully administering God's grace in its various forms* (v. 10).

How did the Lord speak to you today and how did you respond?

_________________________________________________________________

_________________________________________________________________

_________________________________________________________________

_________________________________________________________________

# Week 7: Worry

*May I remember that it is not for me to worry about tomorrow,
but to gladly do Your will this day.*

Christ said:

> "So do not worry, saying, 'What shall we eat?' or 'What shall we drink?' or 'What shall we wear?' For the [unbelievers] run after all these things, and your heavenly Father knows that you need them. But seek first his kingdom and his righteousness, and all these things will be given to you as well."

Matthew 6:31-33 (NIV)

These words of Jesus tell us that we remove worry not by our own strength, but by seeking God's kingdom and His righteousness.

> With regard to the problem that is pressing in on you right now, are you "fixing your eyes on Jesus" (Hebrews 12:2) and receiving peace from Him? If so, He will be a gracious blessing of peace exhibited in and through you. But if you try to worry your way out of the problem, you destroy His effectiveness in you…. When a person confers with Jesus Christ, the confusion stops, because there is no confusion in Him.
>
> —Oswald Chambers [6]

From my first recollections as a child I always wanted to do things well, to be in control of situations so that no unexpected circumstances would upset my plans, and most of all to do things my way. These characteristics can be very beneficial in our society and often lead to success in this world, but the flip side is a propensity to worry.

Since coming to know the Lord, I have often wished that He would just switch off my old way of thinking and switch on a full measure of His presence, but that is not how the Lord works. He wants us to yield to Him by our own choices and draw daily closer to Him and in so doing lose our fears and worries.

In this process, which can be long and painful, we need to continuously recognize how great, mighty and awesome our Lord is, and I penned these simple phrases to remind me of this truth.

WHY SO FEARFUL?
> Why so fearful, oh, my heart?
> The Lord is my comfort and my confidence: the great and mighty God!
>
> Why so fearful, oh, my soul?
> The Lord is my rock and my refuge: the great and awesome God!
>
> Why so fearful, oh, my mind?
> The Lord is my shield and my strength: the great, mighty and awesome God!

## Reflections and Questions

What situations make you worry?

Do these worries spill over into other parts of your life and affect your relationship with other people and your witness for Jesus Christ?

## *Challenge for This Week*

As you read the passages of scripture this week, also pray that the Lord will show you how to build your faith in Him so that the things you worry about diminish.

---

## *Memory Verse*

Cast all your anxiety on him because he cares for you.

1 Peter 5:7

---

## *Readings for Week 7: Worry*

Day 1 (__/__/__) - Psalm 55:1-8, 16-19 and 22-23

Key verse: *Cast your cares on the LORD and he will sustain you; he will never let the righteous fall* (v. 22).

How did the Lord speak to you today and how did you respond?

_______________________________________________

_______________________________________________

_______________________________________________

_______________________________________________

Day 2 (__/__/__) - Psalm 143:1-12

Key verse: *Teach me to do your will, for you are my God; may your good Spirit lead me on level ground* (v. 10).

How did the Lord speak to you today and how did you respond?

_______________________________________________

_______________________________________________

_______________________________________________

_______________________________________________

Day 3 (__/__/__) - Matthew 6:25-34

Key verse: *"Therefore do not worry about tomorrow, for tomorrow will worry about itself. Each day has enough trouble of its own"* (v. 34).

How did the Lord speak to you today and how did you respond?

_______________________________________________

_______________________________________________

_______________________________________________

_______________________________________________

Day 4 (__/__/__) - Mark 4:1-8 and 13-20

    Key verse: *"Still others, like seed sown among thorns, hear the word; but the worries of this life,…come in and choke the word, making it unfruitful"* (vv. 18, 19).

How did the Lord speak to you today and how did you respond?

______________________________________________________

______________________________________________________

______________________________________________________

______________________________________________________

Day 5 (__/__/__) - Luke 21:5-36

    Key verse: *"Be careful, or your hearts will be weighed down with … the anxieties of life, and that day will close on you unexpectedly like a trap"* (v. 34).

How did the Lord speak to you today and how did you respond?

______________________________________________________

______________________________________________________

______________________________________________________

______________________________________________________

Day 6 (__/__/__) - 1 Peter 5:6-11

    Key verse: *Cast all your anxiety on him because he cares for you* (v. 7).

How did the Lord speak to you today and how did you respond?

______________________________________________________

______________________________________________________

______________________________________________________

______________________________________________________

# Week 8: Peace

## *May I know the peace and confidence that comes from following Your way.*

The Lord tells us in Isaiah 32:17, "The fruit of righteousness will be peace; the effect of righteousness will be quietness and confidence forever." Consequently, to find this peace of mind and confidence that the Lord promises, we must find righteousness—we must be "right" with the Lord.

> When man was created he was at peace with God, with himself, and with his fellow humans. But when he rebelled against God, his fellowship with God was broken. He was no longer at peace with himself. And he was no longer at peace with others.
>
> Can these dimensions of peace ever be restored? The Bible says yes. It tells us man alone cannot do what is necessary to heal the brokenness in his relationships—but God can, and has.
>
> *—Billy Graham* [7]

I had made a bad decision in selling a car that resulted in the title of the vehicle remaining in my name even as I had lost contact with the person I had sold it to, and he was involved in a hit-and-run accident and multiple parking offenses. This was a time of great stress for my wife and me as we faced the challenges of the police investigation, insurance claims, parking fines, and trying to resolve the problem with the local Department of Motor Vehicles. But as hard as we tried to resolve the issue, nothing happened and we remained liable for all the offenses.

The height of the crisis corresponded with the time we had made arrangements to take a one-week vacation in Yellowstone National Park, and we seriously considered cancelling our vacation and spending our time searching for the car I had sold and the person who was creating this mayhem for us. However, the Lord placed on our hearts to proceed with the vacation, and so we found His peace.

However, as we returned from the vacation the stress also inevitably returned, but a still small voice in my mind said, "Go back to the DMV", and as we did so we found that the records had been changed so that the title was now in the name of 'persons unknown'. God's grace had worked in an amazing, providential way to start us on the road to resolving all the problems. This inspired me to write this one-sentence poem that I often return to to reconnect with my Lord and His peace and grace.

HIS PEACE
> Know His peace,
> know His pace,
> by His Spirit,
> by His grace.

## Reflections and Questions

In what situations do you have stress instead of peace, frustration instead of quietness, and feelings of inadequacy instead of confidence?

## Challenge for This Week

As you read the daily scriptures this week, also pray to Jesus for the faith to release all difficult situations to Him so that you would know the peace of God.

## Memory Verse

The fruit of righteousness will be peace; the effect of righteousness will be quietness and confidence forever.

Isaiah 32:17

## Readings for Week 8: Peace

Day 1 (__/__/__) - Proverbs 3:21-26

Key verse: *Have no fear of sudden disaster or of the ruin that overtakes the wicked, for the LORD will be your confidence and will keep your foot from being snared* (vv. 25-26).

How did the Lord speak to you today and how did you respond?

__________________________________________________

__________________________________________________

__________________________________________________

__________________________________________________

Day 2 (__/__/__) - Isaiah 9:2-7

Key verse: *For to us a child is born, to us a son is given, and the government will be on his shoulders. And he will be called Wonderful Counselor, Mighty God, Everlasting Father, Prince of Peace* (v. 6).

How did the Lord speak to you today and how did you respond?

__________________________________________________

__________________________________________________

__________________________________________________

__________________________________________________

Day 3 (__/__/__) - Jeremiah 17:5-8

Key verse: *"But blessed is the man who trusts in the LORD, whose confidence is in him"* (v. 7).

How did the Lord speak to you today and how did you respond?

__________________________________________________

__________________________________________________

__________________________________________________

__________________________________________________

Day 4 (__/__/__) - John 14:15-27
Key verse: *"Peace I leave with you; my peace I give you. I do not give to you as the world gives. Do not let your hearts be troubled and do not be afraid"* (v. 27).

How did the Lord speak to you today and how did you respond?

________________________________________________

________________________________________________

________________________________________________

________________________________________________

Day 5 (__/__/__) - Romans 5:1-11
Key verse: *Therefore, since we have been justified through faith, we have peace with God through our LORD Jesus Christ, …* (v. 1).

How did the Lord speak to you today and how did you respond?

________________________________________________

________________________________________________

________________________________________________

________________________________________________

Day 6 (__/__/__) - Hebrews 12:1-13
Key verse: *No discipline seems pleasant at the time, but painful. Later on, however, it produces a harvest of righteousness and peace for those who have been trained by it* (v. 11).

How did the Lord speak to you today and how did you respond?

________________________________________________

________________________________________________

________________________________________________

________________________________________________

# *Week 9: Joy*

*May I know the joy that springs from this peace as I see You move in the lives of those who love You.*

Joy is one of the fruit of the Spirit that Paul mentions in his letter to the Galatians where he writes, "But the fruit of the Spirit is love, joy, peace, patience, kindness, goodness, faithfulness, gentleness and self-control" (Galatians 5:22-23). These then are the benefits that come to us, and can shine through us as a witness to others, when we follow the Lord's way.

> Why do I not rejoice much more over my holy and faithful Savior, Christ, who gave himself for me and to me wholly as my own? Shame on me because of my unbelief, that my heart is not here full of laughter and eternal joy, when I hear and know how he says to me through his Word that he will be my beloved bridegroom.
>
> *—Martin Luther* [8]

It was a difficult trip from the beginning. The flight out of Houston to Abu Dhabi via New York was cancelled because of snow in New York. After a lengthy delay and rerouting I arrived at my destination only to find that my bags were still in Amsterdam. When I checked into the hotel they put me in a room that was above the main disco bar with music blasting in my ears until 2:00 a.m. in the morning. The next day I arrived at our site office to find the internet connection seemed slower than the U. S. Postal Service, and the relations with our client were at a desperately low level.

In these difficult days I continued in my commitment to daily Bible reading and prayer, and the Lord 'guided' me to passages relating to praise and joy. Through this continued fellowship with our Lord I learned the wonderful lesson that our joy does not depend on our circumstances; rather, our joy depends solely on maintaining our fellowship with Him so that we do not quench the Holy Spirit.

THE JOY OF BUSINESS TRAVEL
> Have joy when your flight gets woefully delayed.
> Have joy when your bags get horribly mislaid.
>
> Have joy when your hotel room is too noisy to sleep.
> Have joy in situations that make you want to weep.
>
> Have joy when your internet connection fails.
> Have joy when your major client bails.
>
> Have joy because God knows all these things.
> Have joy because He will lift you on His wings.

## *Reflections and Questions*

Make an assessment of the extent to which the fruit of the Spirit are present in your life (always, most of the time, sometimes, infrequently, never).

| | | | | | |
|---|---|---|---|---|---|
| Love | __________ | Joy | __________ | Peace | __________ |
| Patience | __________ | Kindness | __________ | Goodness | __________ |
| Faithfulness | __________ | Gentleness | __________ | Self-control | __________ |

## *Challenge for This Week*

In prayer ask Jesus to open your heart to understand what is keeping you from experiencing the full blessings of the Holy Spirit and what actions you need to take to remove these barriers.

### *Memory Verse*

But the fruit of the Spirit is love, joy, peace, patience, kindness, goodness, faithfulness, gentleness and self-control.

Galatians 5:22-23

## *Readings for Week 9: Joy*

Day 1 (__/__/__) - Nehemiah 8:1-18

Key verse: *Nehemiah said, "Go and enjoy choice food and sweet drinks, and send some to those who have nothing prepared. This day is sacred to our Lord. Do not grieve, for the joy of the Lord is your strength."* (v. 10).

How did the Lord speak to you today and how did you respond?

__________________________________________________

__________________________________________________

__________________________________________________

__________________________________________________

Day 2 (__/__/__) - Psalm 95:1-11

Key verse: *Come, let us sing for joy to the Lord; let us shout aloud to the Rock of our salvation* (v. 1).

How did the Lord speak to you today and how did you respond?

__________________________________________________

__________________________________________________

__________________________________________________

__________________________________________________

Day 3 (__/__/__) - Psalm 100:1-5
Key verse: *Worship the LORD with gladness; come before him with joyful songs* (v. 2).

How did the Lord speak to you today and how did you respond?

_______________________________________________

_______________________________________________

_______________________________________________

_______________________________________________

Day 4 (__/__/__) - Isaiah 55:8-13
Key verse: *You will go out in joy and be led forth in peace; the mountains and hills will burst into song before you, and all the trees of the field will clap their hands* (v. 12).

How did the Lord speak to you today and how did you respond?

_______________________________________________

_______________________________________________

_______________________________________________

_______________________________________________

Day 5 (__/__/__) - John 15:1-17
Key verse: *"I have told you this so that my joy may be in you and that your joy may be complete"* (v. 11).

How did the Lord speak to you today and how did you respond?

_______________________________________________

_______________________________________________

_______________________________________________

_______________________________________________

Day 6 (__/__/__) - James 1:2-8
Key verse: *Consider it pure joy, my brothers, whenever you face trials of many kinds, …* (v. 2).

How did the Lord speak to you today and how did you respond?

_______________________________________________

_______________________________________________

_______________________________________________

_______________________________________________

# Week 10: Prayer

## May I know that all of this is possible as I pray and give praise in all things.

How is it possible to live in the Lord's way in a world that has values that contradict the values of our Lord in almost every instance?

By our own strength it is not possible. Only when we commit our lives to the Lord—communicating with Him daily through the Bible and through prayer—can His truth be manifested in our lives. As Paul said, "Be joyful always; pray continually; give thanks in all circumstances, for this is God's will for you in Christ Jesus" (1 Thessalonians 5:16-18).

> When a general chooses the place from which he intends to strike the enemy, he pays the most attention to those points he thinks most important in the fight. On the battlefield of Waterloo there was a farmhouse which Wellington immediately saw as the key to the situation. He did not spare his troops in his endeavor to hold that point: the victory depended on it. So it actually happened. It is the same in the conflict between the believer and the powers of darkness. The place of private prayer is the key, the strategic position where decisive victory is obtained.
>
> —*Andrew Murray* [9]

Just as our interaction with a dear friend can take on many forms, so our interaction in prayer with our Dearest Friend should take on many forms. Take time to read the writing below together with the referenced Bible verses and the Holy Spirit will open new vistas to an expanded and enriched time of prayer with our Lord.

THE BEAUTIFUL GIFT OF PRAYER

Thank you, Father, for the beautiful gift of prayer:

Thank You for prayer in solitude … (cf Matthew 6:6)
Thank You for prayer with other believers … (cf Acts 1:14)
Thank You for prayer in the details of life … (cf Philippians 4:6)
Thank You for prayer in the important decisions of life … (cf Luke 6:12-13)
Thank You for prayer at the start of the day … (cf Mark 1:35)
Thank You for prayer at the end of the day … (cf Matthew 14:23)
Thank You for prayer with joy … (cf Philippians 1:3-5)
Thank You for prayer with anguish … (cf Mark 14:34-36)
Thank You for prayer with certainty … (cf Mark 11:24)
Thank You for prayer with doubt … (cf Romans 8:26)
Thank You for prayer by many … (cf 2 Corinthians 1:10b-11)
Thank You for prayer by few … (cf James 5:16b)
Thank You for prayer with fellowship … (cf Acts 2:42)
Thank You for prayer with fasting … (cf Acts 14:23)
Thank You for prayer in all things … (cf 1 Thessalonians 5:16-18)

Thank you, Father, for this beautiful gift of prayer.

## *Reflections and Questions*

If you have been meeting daily with our Lord in His Word and in prayer for the last ten weeks you will have seen God blessing your life in various ways. Identify some of these blessings.

If you have been unable to meet daily with our Lord identify the barriers that prevent you from doing this.

## *Challenge for This Week*

The beginning and the end of making the changes in our lives—to resolve our fears and to be a true witness for Him—is a closer walk with Jesus. Think and pray about any barriers in your life that need to be removed to have this closer walk with our Savior.

### *Memory Verse*

Be joyful always; pray continually; give thanks in all circumstances, for this is God's will for you in Christ Jesus.

1 Thessalonians 5:16-18

## *Readings for Week 10: Prayer*

Day 1 (__/__/__) - Psalm 17:1-15

Key verse: *I call on you, O God, for you will answer me; give ear to me and hear my prayer* (v. 6).

How did the Lord speak to you today and how did you respond?

___________________________________________________

___________________________________________________

___________________________________________________

___________________________________________________

Day 2 (__/__/__) - Matthew 6:5-15

Key verse: *"But when you pray, go into your room, close the door and pray to your Father, who is unseen. Then your Father, who sees what is done in secret, will reward you"* (v. 6).

How did the Lord speak to you today and how did you respond?

___________________________________________________

___________________________________________________

___________________________________________________

___________________________________________________

Day 3 (__/__/__) - Luke 18:1-14

Key verse: *Then Jesus told his disciples a parable to show them that they should always pray and not give up* (v. 1).

How did the Lord speak to you today and how did you respond?

____________________________________________________________

____________________________________________________________

____________________________________________________________

____________________________________________________________

Day 4 (__/__/__) - Luke 22:39-46

Key verse: *And being in anguish, he prayed more earnestly, and his sweat was like drops of blood falling to the ground* (v. 44).

How did the Lord speak to you today and how did you respond?

____________________________________________________________

____________________________________________________________

____________________________________________________________

____________________________________________________________

Day 5 (__/__/__) - Colossians 4:2-6

Key verse: *Devote yourselves to prayer, being watchful and thankful* (v. 2).

How did the Lord speak to you today and how did you respond?

____________________________________________________________

____________________________________________________________

____________________________________________________________

____________________________________________________________

Day 6 (__/__/__) - James 5:13-20

Key verse: *The prayer of a righteous man is powerful and effective* (v. 16b).

How did the Lord speak to you today and how did you respond?

____________________________________________________________

____________________________________________________________

____________________________________________________________

____________________________________________________________

# Part II: Abide in Him

Oh how difficult it is to abide in the Lord: difficult in times of great activity and difficult in times of low activity, difficult in times of forward progress and difficult in times of frustration, difficult in times of being honored and difficult in times of being criticized. But we must try.

**To abide** in Him is to recognize the deceit in our hearts.
**To abide** in Him is to recognize the love and power available by allowing the Spirit of Christ to flow into our hearts.

**To abide** in Him is to work diligently and responsibly for the Lord.
**To abide** in Him is to wait quietly on the Lord.

**To abide** in Him is to know that the pathway He blocks no one can clear.
**To abide** in Him is to know that the doors He opens no one can shut.

**To abide** in Him is to suffer through many trials and hardships.
**To abide** in Him is to know that the Lord will not let us be tempted beyond what we can endure.

And if we try, we find that His yoke is easy and His burden is light, as all things do work together for those who love God.

Amen.

When we belong to the Lord and earnestly seek His way, He is not content for us only to follow a set of Christian principles; He wants us to abide in Him. Jesus makes this clear in John 15:4 where He says, "Abide in Me, and I in you. As the branch cannot bear fruit of itself, unless it abides in the vine, so neither can you, unless you abide in Me" (NASB).

# Week 11: Our Deceitful Hearts

## To abide in Him is to recognize the deceit in our hearts.

One of the most painful steps to take in learning to abide in Christ is to recognize that we are deceitful by nature. We justify our worldly natures in a spirit of pride and defiance against the written word of God and the nudging of our consciences. Christ leaves no doubt about this when He says, "For from within, out of men's hearts, come evil thoughts, sexual immorality, theft, murder, adultery, greed, malice, deceit, lewdness, envy, slander, arrogance and folly" (Mark 7:21-22).

> There is one vice of which no man in the world is free; which everyone in the world loathes when he sees it in someone else; and of which hardly any people, except Christians, even imagine they are guilty themselves. ….
>
> The vice I am talking about is Pride or Self-Conceit. …. Unchastity, anger, greed, drunkenness, and all that, are mere fleabites in comparison: it was through Pride that the devil became the devil: Pride leads to every other vice: it is the complete anti-God state of mind.
>
> —*C. S. Lewis* [10]

At the time I came to know the Lord and for two years thereafter we lived in Santa Barbara, California, and very early each Saturday morning I would take our son for a long walk along a quiet beach on the west side of town. This beach had many rock pools and abundant life in the deeper waters that would yield a bumper crop of sea shells for most of our visits. Also I quickly realized that the largest and most difficult to find shells would be washed up onto the beach after a storm: the stronger the storm, the bigger the harvest of these beautiful shells.

Our walk with the Lord is like this as well. It is often after a crisis or major problem in our lives that the Lord provides us with some beautiful insight that draws us closer to Him. It was after one such crisis that the Lord revealed to me there was sin and deceit in my life which was so much part of me I desperately wanted to hold onto it. Therefore, I needed to ask Jesus to tear away this sin as I could not readily yield it to the urgings of His Spirit. The storm was not easy but the revelation and release were gems to find and treasures to keep as captured in this prayer.

THAT I MAY LOVE YOU MORE
    Dear Lord Jesus,
    Show me who I am,
    that I may know You more,
    that I may love You more.

    Take away my sins,
    that I may know You more,
    that I may love You more.

    Tear away my sins,
    that I may know You more,
    that I may love You more.

    Leave only Your Spirit,
    that I may know You more,
    that I may love You more.

That I may know You more,
that I may love You more.
Amen.

## Reflections and Questions

Are there things in your life that you know are not right with God, but you have trouble releasing to Him? Are there things that you enjoy doing in your own strength or enjoy receiving compliments about from other people, but in your heart you know they do not honor God?

## Challenge for This Week

As you read the scriptures and pray this week seek to surrender all things to Jesus Christ so that you may see the fullness of the deceit in your heart and release more of your worldly nature to His presence.

---

### Memory Verse

The heart is deceitful above all things and beyond cure. Who can understand it?

Jeremiah 17:9

---

## Readings for Week 11: Our Deceitful Hearts

Day 1 (__/__/__) - Genesis 6:1-8

Key verse: *The LORD saw how great man's wickedness on the earth had become, and that every inclination of the thoughts of his heart was only evil all the time* (v. 5).

How did the Lord speak to you today and how did you respond?

__________________________________________

__________________________________________

__________________________________________

__________________________________________

Day 2 (__/__/__) - Genesis 8:15-22

Key verse: *The LORD smelled the pleasing aroma and said in his heart: "Never again will I curse the ground because of man, even though every inclination of his heart is evil from childhood"* (v. 21a).

How did the Lord speak to you today and how did you respond?

__________________________________________

__________________________________________

__________________________________________

__________________________________________

Day 3 (__/__/__) - Jeremiah 17:5-10
   Key verse: *The heart is deceitful above all things and beyond cure. Who can understand it? (v. 9).*

How did the Lord speak to you today and how did you respond?

_______________________________________________________________________

_______________________________________________________________________

_______________________________________________________________________

_______________________________________________________________________


Day 4 (__/__/__) - Mark 7:1-23
   Key verse: *"For from within, out of men's hearts, come evil thoughts, sexual immorality, theft, murder, adultery, greed, malice, deceit, lewdness, envy, slander, arrogance and folly"* (vv. 21-22).

How did the Lord speak to you today and how did you respond?

_______________________________________________________________________

_______________________________________________________________________

_______________________________________________________________________

_______________________________________________________________________


Day 5 (__/__/__) - Galatians 5:16-21
   Key verse: *For the sinful nature desires what is contrary to the Spirit, and the Spirit what is contrary to the sinful nature (v. 17a).*

How did the Lord speak to you today and how did you respond?

_______________________________________________________________________

_______________________________________________________________________

_______________________________________________________________________

_______________________________________________________________________


Day 6 (__/__/__) - Colossians 3:1-11
   Key verse: *Put to death, therefore, whatever belongs to your earthly nature: sexual immorality, impurity, lust, evil desires and greed, which is idolatry (v. 5).*

How did the Lord speak to you today and how did you respond?

_______________________________________________________________________

_______________________________________________________________________

_______________________________________________________________________

_______________________________________________________________________

# *Week 12: Christ's Love and Power*

*To abide in Him is to recognize the love and power available
by allowing the Spirit of Christ to flow into our hearts.*

Once we acknowledge and repent of our sinful natures, the Lord does not leave us without recourse. On the contrary, He promises and provides us with much greater strength, both in love toward our fellow men and in power to carry out our responsibilities. Paul describes this in his letter to Timothy where he writes, "For God did not give us a spirit of timidity, but a spirit of power, of love and of self-discipline" (2 Timothy 1:7).

Jesus instructs us to pray, "Your kingdom come." By this prayer we are taking our role as members of a race who once betrayed the King and forfeited His intended purposes into the claws of the adversary. But now, as His redeemed sons and daughters, He has endowed us with restored "kingdom authority," through prayer to welcome His entry into every need and pain of this planet.

The power is God's, but the privilege and responsibility to pray are ours. So, let us hear and understand Jesus' words and come together at His throne, expecting and receiving the flow of the Holy Spirit's power.

*—Jack W. Hayford* [11]

Eighteen to twenty miles into a marathon the runners often 'hit the wall' when they deplete their bodies of glycogen, the main source of energy for strenuous exercise, and they quickly experience serious fatigue. This phase of the race really test the runners' endurance as they must start burning stored fat, which does not burn so readily as the glycogen, and the temptation to drop out of the race is very strong.

I experienced this phenomenon of 'hitting the wall' in my walk with the Lord. After I had followed my Savior as faithfully as I could for nineteen years, I suddenly felt that I could not go on and my steps became slow and labored. In this struggle the Lord whispered to my spirit that my energy may be depleted but His tank of energy was always full and available to all who believed. Soon I was able to say to my Lord, "Lead me on!"

LEAD ME ON

Lead me on, Lord Jesus, lead me on!

Make my feet like the feet of a deer, to enable me to go on the heights. Broaden the path beneath me so that my ankles do not turn.
Lead me on, Lord Jesus, lead me on!

Renew my strength so that I can soar on wings like an eagle, so that I can run and not grow weary, walk and not be faint.
Lead me on, Lord Jesus, lead me on!

Help me strain toward what is ahead; to press on toward the goal to win the prize for which You have called me heavenward.
Lead me on, Lord Jesus, lead me on!

## *Reflections and Questions*

When have you felt the Spirit of God powerfully intervene in your life? Also when have you lacked power, love, or self-discipline from the Spirit of God?

## Challenge for This Week

Ask God that you may not only overcome your weaknesses, but that you may also be filled with His power to live as He would have you live.

### Memory Verse

For God did not give us a spirit of timidity, but a spirit of power, of love and of self-discipline.

2 Timothy 1:7

## Readings for Week 12: Christ's Love and Power

Day 1 (__/__/__) - Luke 24:36-49

Key verse: *"I am going to send you what my Father has promised; but stay in the city until you have been clothed with power from on high"* (v. 49).

How did the Lord speak to you today and how did you respond?

_______________________________________________

_______________________________________________

_______________________________________________

_______________________________________________

Day 2 (__/__/__) - Acts 1:1-11

Key verse: *"But you will receive power when the Holy Spirit comes on you; and you will be my witnesses…to the ends of the earth"* (v. 8).

How did the Lord speak to you today and how did you respond?

_______________________________________________

_______________________________________________

_______________________________________________

_______________________________________________

Day 3 (__/__/__) - 2 Corinthians 13:1-10

Key verse: *For to be sure, he was crucified in weakness, yet he lives by God's power. Likewise, we are weak in him, yet by God's power we will live with him to serve you* (v. 4).

How did the Lord speak to you today and how did you respond?

_______________________________________________

_______________________________________________

_______________________________________________

_______________________________________________

Day 4 (__/__/__) - Ephesians 3:14-21
    Key verse: *I pray that out of his glorious riches he may strengthen you with power through his Spirit in your inner being, …* (v. 16).

How did the Lord speak to you today and how did you respond?

______________________________________________

______________________________________________

______________________________________________

______________________________________________

Day 5 (__/__/__) - 1 Thessalonians 1:2-10
    Key verse: *…, because our gospel came to you not simply with words, but also with power, with the Holy Spirit and with deep conviction* (v. 5a).

How did the Lord speak to you today and how did you respond?

______________________________________________

______________________________________________

______________________________________________

______________________________________________

Day 6 (__/__/__) - 2 Peter 1:3-11
    Key verse: *His divine power has given us everything we need for life and godliness through our knowledge of him who called us by his own glory and goodness* (v. 3).

How did the Lord speak to you today and how did you respond?

______________________________________________

______________________________________________

______________________________________________

______________________________________________

# *Week 13: Work*

## *To abide in Him is to work diligently and responsibly for the Lord.*

Work has been a vital part of man's relationship with God ever since He created Adam. Consequently, our work, regardless of its nature, is an expression of God's will for us.

Nevertheless, God has given us a free choice: to work as working for Him or to work as working for ourselves. And Paul makes it very clear which choice we should make: "Whatever you do, work at it with all your heart, as working for the Lord, not for men, since you know that you will receive an inheritance from the Lord as a reward. It is the Lord Christ you are serving" (Colossians 3:23-24).

> God uses everything in the workplace to train our character. He uses the evil we face, the people we can't stand, the circumstances of tension and pressure, the tedium of long afternoons, the solicitations to compromise, the irritations of angry customers, the interruptions, the financial reversals, the deals that fall through, even the traffic on the way home—He uses all of it to make us like Jesus.
>
> *—Doug Sherman and William Hendricks* [12]

I had worked in the oil industry for over fifteen years and it concerned me that so many people were not excited and motivated in their work life. Eventually, I wrote a book on this topic, which was soundly rejected by publishers and literary agents alike, but the yearning remained. It led me to leave my job to focus on this passion. However, my own writing skills soon dried up and in desperation I turned to the Lord. I then remained in 'the school of my Lord' for two years soaking up knowledge of Him and writing about Him, but when this period came to an end, instead of granting my heart's desire to become a published author and public speaker, He sent me back into the workplace and soon showed me that here was one of His main harvest fields.

It took me a long time to gain a good understanding of how to live for Christ in the secular workplace, but I eventually learned that each trial and frustration had kingdom opportunities to witness of His presence and His love.

THE BLESSINGS OF WORK

Think of work as a blessed task …
because through the trials of work we are drawn closer to God.

Think of work as a vibrant opportunity …
because by our attitude to work we can spread the fragrance of the knowledge of Jesus to those who are lost.

Think of work as having eternal significance …
because we can shine like stars in the universe at work as we hold out the word of life to those who need Jesus.

## *Reflections and Questions*

Think of the times when you are able to work "as working for the Lord." How does this differ from the times when you struggle?

## *Challenge for This Week*

In prayer continue to seek that closer walk with Jesus and the presence of His Spirit that you may have the desire, patience, and perseverance to always see your work as serving Him.

## *Memory Verse*

Whatever you do, work at it with all your heart, as working for the Lord, not for men, since you know that you will receive an inheritance from the Lord as a reward. It is the Lord Christ you are serving.

Colossians 3:23-24

## *Readings for Week 13: Work*

Day 1 (__/__/__) - Genesis 2:4-17

Key verse: *The LORD God took the man and put him in the Garden of Eden to work it and take care of it* (v. 15).

How did the Lord speak to you today and how did you respond?

_______________________________________________

_______________________________________________

_______________________________________________

_______________________________________________

Day 2 (__/__/__) - Genesis 3:17-24

Key verse: *To Adam he said,… "Cursed is the ground because of you; through painful toil you will eat of it all the days of your life"* (v. 17).

How did the Lord speak to you today and how did you respond?

_______________________________________________

_______________________________________________

_______________________________________________

_______________________________________________

Day 3 (__/__/__) - Ecclesiastes 2:17-26

Key verse: *A man can do nothing better than to eat and drink and find satisfaction in his work. This too, I see, is from the hand of God, for without him, who can eat or find enjoyment?* (vv. 24-25).

How did the Lord speak to you today and how did you respond?

_______________________________________________

_______________________________________________

_______________________________________________

_______________________________________________

Day 4 (__/__/__) - Matthew 25:14-30

Key verse: *"His master replied, 'Well done, good and faithful servant! You have been faithful with a few things; I will put you in charge of many things'"* (v. 21a).

How did the Lord speak to you today and how did you respond?

_______________________________________________

_______________________________________________

_______________________________________________

_______________________________________________

Day 5 (__/__/__) - John 6:25-40

Key verse: *"Do not work for food that spoils, but for food that endures to eternal life, which the Son of Man will give you"* (v. 27a).

How did the Lord speak to you today and how did you respond?

_______________________________________________

_______________________________________________

_______________________________________________

_______________________________________________

Day 6 (__/__/__) - Ephesians 6:5-8

Key verse: *Serve wholeheartedly, as if you were serving the LORD, not men, ...* (v. 7).

How did the Lord speak to you today and how did you respond?

_______________________________________________

_______________________________________________

_______________________________________________

_______________________________________________

# Week 14: Waiting

## To abide in Him is to wait quietly on the Lord.

One of the hardest things to do is to wait quietly on the Lord, especially when we seem to stagnate as others succeed and pass us by. But in Psalm 37:7 David speaks clearly to us and gives us hope, "Be still before the LORD and wait patiently for him; do not fret when men succeed in their ways...."

> It is hard to be called by God and live in our society at the same time. In America, when the action impulse comes, action follows immediately. No patience required—technology and culture let us proceed immediately. Not so with God. Immediately when He calls us, He postpones our sending. There is other work to be done first.
>
> —*Patrick M. Morley* [13]

Exodus 40:36-38 tells us, "In all the travels of the Israelites, whenever the cloud lifted from above the tabernacle, they would set out; but if the cloud did not lift, they did not set out—until the day it lifted. So the cloud of the Lord was over the tabernacle by day, and fire was in the cloud by night, in the sight of all the house of Israel during all their travels."

Oh how frustrating it must have been for the Israelites not to move at their own pace to the Promised Land. I can imagine a beautiful clear day in the Sinai Peninsula that was ideal for travelling but the pillar of cloud didn't budge. Maybe that one day turned into a week or even a month and still the cloud showed no signs of movement—how they must have murmured against the Lord, but to no avail.

I confess that I have frequently been like the Israelites, thinking I know much better than my Lord the path that I should take, the times when I should be moving forward, and the times when I should be holding back. However, the cloud of His Presence, now the Holy Spirit living in us, has never been moved by my meager agenda, but only by His perfect agenda for my life to bring Him the glory.

BE STILL

I sought to do God's will, and God said, "Be still."

I tried to accomplish the plans I had laid out, but God said, "Be still."

I sought all manner of ways and all types of advice to achieve my goals, but God said, "Be still."

I pined over the glory of past accomplishments; I paced the room like a caged animal; I cried out to the Lord, "This cannot be your will!" But the Lord said, "Be still."

## Reflections and Questions

Where do you see that you have lost ground to others, or may lose ground to others, by waiting for the Lord?

## Challenge for This Week

Much prayer and support from fellow believers is needed to take us through one of the hardest parts of our growth in the Lord—waiting for Him. Always be diligent in prayer, faithful in reading His Word, and unashamed in seeking support from fellow believers.

## *Memory Verse*

Wait for the LORD; be strong and take heart and wait for the LORD.

Psalm 27:14

## *Readings for Week 14: Waiting*

Day 1 (__/__/__) - Psalm 27:1-14
Key verse: *Wait for the LORD; be strong and take heart and wait for the LORD* (v. 14).

How did the Lord speak to you today and how did you respond?

_______________________________________________________

_______________________________________________________

_______________________________________________________

_______________________________________________________

Day 2 (__/__/__) - Psalm 37:1-40
Key verse: *Be still before the LORD and wait patiently for him; do not fret when men succeed in their ways, when they carry out their wicked schemes* (v. 7).

How did the Lord speak to you today and how did you respond?

_______________________________________________________

_______________________________________________________

_______________________________________________________

_______________________________________________________

Day 3 (__/__/__) - Psalm 46:1-11
Key verse: *"Be still, and know that I am God; …"* (v. 10a).

How did the Lord speak to you today and how did you respond?

_______________________________________________________

_______________________________________________________

_______________________________________________________

_______________________________________________________

Day 4 (__/__/__) - Psalm 130:1-6
   Key verse: *I wait for the LORD, my soul waits, and in his word I put my hope* (v. 5).

How did the Lord speak to you today and how did you respond?

______________________________________________________

______________________________________________________

______________________________________________________

______________________________________________________


Day 5 (__/__/__) - Hebrews 6:13-20
   Key verse: *And so after waiting patiently, Abraham received what was promised* (v. 15).

How did the Lord speak to you today and how did you respond?

______________________________________________________

______________________________________________________

______________________________________________________

______________________________________________________


Day 6 (__/__/__) - 2 Peter 3:1-13
   Key verse: *The LORD is not slow in keeping his promise, as some understand slowness. He is patient with you, not wanting anyone to perish, but everyone to come to repentance* (v.9).

How did the Lord speak to you today and how did you respond?

______________________________________________________

______________________________________________________

______________________________________________________

______________________________________________________

# Week 15: Open and Closed Doors

*To abide in Him is to know that the pathway*
*He blocks no one can clear.*
*To abide in Him is to know that the doors*
*He opens no one can shut.*

When we first follow our Savior, we often try to impose our own will as God's will, and this causes us to try to go along paths that the Lord does not intend for us to take. However, if we are faithful, the Lord will soon teach us the lessons of Revelation 3:7, "What he opens no one can shut, and what he shuts no one can open."

> He waits for us to despair of human strength and then intervenes with heavenly. God waits for us to give up and then—surprise!
>
> Has it been a while since you let God surprise you? It's easy to reach a point where [we believe] we have God figured out.
>
> We know exactly what God does. We break the code…
>
> Have you got God figured out? Have you got God captured on a flowchart …? If so, then listen. Listen to God's surprises.
>
> *—Max Lucado* [14]

When the company I worked for moved from California to Houston I had an opportunity to move with them, but I was convinced that the Lord wanted my wife and me to stay in California, as many family members lived close by and I had an emerging leadership position in the prayer ministry at a large church. However, no matter how hard I tried no doors opened for me to be able to earn a living.

After a ten-month search that more than depleted the severance package from the company move, I reluctantly, very reluctantly, called my previous employer in Houston to see if a move to rejoin them was still possible. Quickly doors opened: within six weeks we were living in Houston, I was restored to my previous management position, paid a bonus to move from California as if I had taken the original transfer offer, and my company benefits were restored based on my original start date with the company. So, in effect, I had received a tremendous blessing of having an eight month paid sabbatical from the severance pay when the company moved, to then rejoin the company without penalty. Moreover, the blessings of living in Houston soon became clear to my wife and me and we marveled at the awesome grace of God. He knew which door to keep closed and which door to open. We only needed to open our eyes to His will.

OPEN OUR EYES, LORD

>Open our eyes, Lord,
>to see as You see.
>
>Open our ears, Lord,
>to hear what You say.
>
>Open our mouths, Lord,
>to speak of Your way.

## *Reflections and Questions*

Has a pathway that seemed so clear and right to you been blocked so that, try as you might, it has been impossible to go forward?

Has a door of opportunity unexpectedly and wonderfully opened up for you where there was no doubt in your mind that this was by the hand of God?

What has the Lord shown you in these situations or, if you have not experienced the Lord's leading in this way, why do you think that is?

## *Challenge for This Week*

God opened and closed doors for Jonah in a most dramatic way (see days one to four of this week's Bible readings). When you read these passages, ask God to open your eyes to see if you are trying to impose your will rather than recognizing His sovereignty.

### *Memory Verse*

What he opens no one can shut, and what he shuts no one can open.

Revelation 3:7b

## *Readings for Week 15: Open and Closed Doors*

Day 1 (__/__/__) - Jonah 1:1-17

Key verse: *But Jonah ran away from the Lord and…sailed for Tarshish to flee from the Lord* (v. 3).

How did the Lord speak to you today and how did you respond?

________________________________________

________________________________________

________________________________________

________________________________________

Day 2 (__/__/__) - Jonah 2:1-10

Key verse: *"In my distress I called to the Lord, and he answered me"* (v. 2a).

How did the Lord speak to you today and how did you respond?

________________________________________

________________________________________

________________________________________

________________________________________

Day 3 (__/__/__) - Jonah 3:1-10
    Key verse: *Jonah obeyed the word of the LORD and went to Nineveh* (v. 3a).

How did the Lord speak to you today and how did you respond?

_______________________________________________

_______________________________________________

_______________________________________________

_______________________________________________

Day 4 (__/__/__) - Jonah 4:1-11
    Key verse: *But Jonah was greatly displeased and became angry [at God]* (v. 1).

How did the Lord speak to you today and how did you respond?

_______________________________________________

_______________________________________________

_______________________________________________

_______________________________________________

Day 5 (__/__/__) - Matthew 7:7-12
    Key verse: *"Ask and it will be given to you; seek and you will find; knock and the door will be opened to you"* (v. 7).

How did the Lord speak to you today and how did you respond?

_______________________________________________

_______________________________________________

_______________________________________________

_______________________________________________

Day 6 (__/__/__) - Revelation 3:7-13
    Key verse: *"I know your deeds. See, I have placed before you an open door that no one can shut"* (v. 8a).

How did the Lord speak to you today and how did you respond?

_______________________________________________

_______________________________________________

_______________________________________________

_______________________________________________

# Week 16: Suffering

## *To abide in Him is to suffer through many trials and hardships.*

Our old nature has such a strong hold on us, and we are so comfortable with it that we cannot abide in Him unless we are driven helpless into Christ's arms. Paul expressed this as he wrote, "We were under great pressure, far beyond our ability to endure… But this happened that we might not rely on ourselves but on God…" (2 Corinthians 1:8-9).

> Biblical teaching and personal experience thus combine to teach that suffering is the path to holiness or maturity. There is always an indefinable something about people who have suffered. They have a fragrance which others lack. They exhibit the meekness and gentleness of Christ.
>
> —*John R. W. Stott* [15]

When we think of suffering the first thoughts are typically: chronic illness, loss of someone who is near and dear, a soldier in the front lines of battle, starving children in a third-world country. But there is also another kind of suffering that can be just as severe, and that is the suffering from the spiritual battle in the mind. The world and our own perspective of living in the world—that is to say, our unredeemed or sinful nature—are so real and immediate that to allow them to be changed by abiding in Jesus and knowing the living presence of the Holy Spirit results in intense spiritual battles where, at times, it seems that the Lord has abandoned us.

CROSSING THE DESERT

O Lord, why are You so far off? I am like a wanderer in the desert knowing only a mirage of Your Spirit.

O Lord, come soon, so that I may reach the refreshing oasis of Your touch.

May I not be put to shame; may others not be able to say, "He searched in vain to follow the Lord."

But if we are faithful, and at times it may seem that our faith is so weak that we are barely holding onto our Lord by our fingernails, we see that He never abandons us and we take another step closer to a full life in Christ as a result of this suffering.

## *Reflections and Questions*

True Christianity is not a broad and easy path, and by now you will have experienced situations in your walk with Jesus that have truly challenged your faith. Identify these situations.

Also, suffering through trials and hardships can, if we are faithful, produce a harvest of righteousness in drawing closer to Jesus Christ. Think about some of these blessings of your walk with our Savior.

## *Challenge for This Week*

Always stay close to our Savior in prayer and in reading His Word, even if you do not sense the Lord's presence. Remember, God calls us to be faithful as an act of will, if necessary, overcoming our emotions by our choices.

## *Memory Verse*

But rejoice that you participate in the sufferings of Christ, so that you may be overjoyed when his glory is revealed.

1 Peter 4:13

## *Readings for Week 16: Suffering*

Day 1 (__/__/__) - Psalm 119:49-80

Key verse: *My comfort in my suffering is this: Your promise preserves my life* (v. 50).

How did the Lord speak to you today and how did you respond?

_______________________________________________

_______________________________________________

_______________________________________________

_______________________________________________

Day 2 (__/__/__) - Matthew 7:13-14 and 24-29

Key verse: *"But small is the gate and narrow the road that leads to life, and only a few find it"* (v. 14).

How did the Lord speak to you today and how did you respond?

_______________________________________________

_______________________________________________

_______________________________________________

_______________________________________________

Day 3 (__/__/__) - 2 Corinthians 1:3-11

Key verse: *For just as the sufferings of Christ flow over into our lives, so also through Christ our comfort over-flows* (v. 5).

How did the Lord speak to you today and how did you respond?

_______________________________________________

_______________________________________________

_______________________________________________

_______________________________________________

Day 4 (__/__/__) - Philippians 3:1-11

Key verse: *What is more, I consider everything a loss compared to the surpassing greatness of knowing Christ Jesus my LORD, for whose sake I have lost all things. I consider them rubbish, that I may gain Christ...* (v. 8).

How did the Lord speak to you today and how did you respond?

_______________________________________________________________

_______________________________________________________________

_______________________________________________________________

_______________________________________________________________

Day 5 (__/__/__) - 1 Peter 1:3-12

Key verse: *These [trials] have come so that your faith...may be proved genuine and may result in praise, glory and honor when Jesus Christ is revealed* (v. 7).

How did the Lord speak to you today and how did you respond?

_______________________________________________________________

_______________________________________________________________

_______________________________________________________________

_______________________________________________________________

Day 6 (__/__/__) - 1 Peter 4:12-19

Key verse: *But rejoice that you participate in the sufferings of Christ, so that you may be overjoyed when his glory is revealed* (v. 13).

How did the Lord speak to you today and how did you respond?

_______________________________________________________________

_______________________________________________________________

_______________________________________________________________

_______________________________________________________________

# Week 17: Temptation



*To abide in Him is to know that the Lord will not let us be tempted beyond what we can endure.*

Often the way is so hard that it seems that it could not be God's will for us to suffer so much, or it seems that we do not have the faith to go on. However, "No temptation has seized you except what is common to man. And God is faithful; he will not let you be tempted beyond what you can bear. But when you are tempted, he will also provide a way out so that you can stand up under it" (1 Corinthians 10:13).

> Satan will most thoroughly and carefully examine us, and if he shall find us to be, like Achilles, vulnerable nowhere else but in our heel, he will shoot his arrows at our heel.
>
> I believe that Satan seldom attacks a man in a place of strength, but he generally looks for a weak point, the besetting sin. "There," says he, "there will I strike the blow." God help us in the hour of battle and the time of conflict! Indeed, unless the Lord should help us, this crafty foe might easily find enough joints in our armor and soon send the deadly arrow into our soul, so that we should fall down wounded before him.
>
> —*Charles Spurgeon* [16]

A period of intense activity and responsibility occurred in my work life when I was about eight years into my walk with the Lord. I was the Quality Assurance Manager for a company that designed and built floating structures for the offshore oil industry. At the time it was necessary for me to lead the company from a fairly unstructured way of doing business to certification to an international quality standard. The pressures of achieving this goal were intense and at times I would get up at 2:30 in the morning to go to work. During this period I tried to stay close to the Lord in daily Bible reading and prayer, but often it seemed that the Lord did not care about the difficulties I was facing and I wrote …

MY COMPLAINT TO GOD

    I wait for You, Lord,
    maybe not patiently,
    maybe not lovingly,
    but I wait.

    I call on Your Name,
    but it seems as if You do not answer my calls,
    do not respond to my letters,
    do not give me an appointment.

    I pray to You in despair,
    confess my sins as I know them,
    in private to You and to others who believe,
    and yet You remain silent.

    Am I to say, "God is not there!"?
    Am I to say, "I can wait no longer."?

No, I know You are there, Lord,
and I know that You care,
also I know that Your will will be done.
I will wait Lord, but remember Your servant for I am in anguish.

The temptation to turn away from the Lord was great and eventually I had to make a decision as to which was most important to me: to obtain the certification to the schedule set by the president of the company, or to be faithful to my Lord by not quenching His Spirit and retain the fruit of love, joy, peace, patience, kindness, goodness, faithfulness, gentleness and self-control (see Galatians 5:22-23). I chose my Lord and He brought the certification process to a successful conclusion.

## Reflections and Questions

Have you been tempted to turn away from God because you felt He had abandoned you in suffering? Have you been tempted to turn away from God because of the enticements of the world and the flesh?

## Challenge for This Week

As you face the trials and temptations of this week, pray earnestly to know in your heart, your soul, and your mind that not only has Jesus gone before us, but also He is always there with us, however difficult the circumstances of our lives may be.

---

## Memory Verse

No temptation has seized you except what is common to man. And God is faithful; he will not let you be tempted beyond what you can bear. But when you are tempted, he will also provide a way out so that you can stand up under it.

1 Corinthians 10:13

---

## Readings for Week 17: Temptation

Day 1 (__/__/__) - Psalm 34:1-22

Key verse: *A righteous man may have many troubles, but the Lord delivers him from them all; ...* (v. 19).

How did the Lord speak to you today and how did you respond?

_______________________________________________

_______________________________________________

_______________________________________________

_______________________________________________

Day 2 (__/__/__) - Matthew 4:1-11
Key verse: *Jesus said to him, "Away from me, Satan! For it is written: 'Worship the LORD your God, and serve him only'"* (v. 10).

How did the Lord speak to you today and how did you respond?

_______________________________________________

_______________________________________________

_______________________________________________

_______________________________________________

Day 3 (__/__/__) - Ephesians 6:10-18
Key verse: *Therefore put on the full armor of God, so that when the day of evil comes, you may be able to stand your ground, and after you have done everything, to stand* (v. 13).

How did the Lord speak to you today and how did you respond?

_______________________________________________

_______________________________________________

_______________________________________________

_______________________________________________

Day 4 (__/__/__) - 1 Thessalonians 3:1-13
Key verse: *I was afraid that in some way the tempter might have tempted you and our efforts might have been useless* (v. 5b).

How did the Lord speak to you today and how did you respond?

_______________________________________________

_______________________________________________

_______________________________________________

_______________________________________________

Day 5 (__/__/__) - Hebrews 2:5-18
Key verse: *Because he himself suffered when he was tempted, he is able to help those who are being tempted* (v. 18).

How did the Lord speak to you today and how did you respond?

_______________________________________________

_______________________________________________

_______________________________________________

_______________________________________________

Day 6 (__/__/__) - James 1:12-18

Key verse: *When tempted, no one should say, "God is tempting me." For God cannot be tempted by evil, nor does he tempt anyone; but each one is tempted when, by his own evil desire, he is dragged away and enticed* (vv.13-14).

How did the Lord speak to you today and how did you respond?

# Week 18: Things Work Together

*And if we try, we find that His yoke is easy and His burden is light as all things do work together for those who love God.*

What greater gift can we receive than to live with Christ in this life? "Come to me, all you who are weary and burdened, and I will give you rest. Take my yoke upon you and learn from me, for I am gentle and humble in heart, and you will find rest for your souls. For my yoke is easy and my burden is light" (Matthew 11:28-30). Then, as we continue to live with Him, we can know and experience that, "God causes all things to work together for good to those who love God, to those who are called according to His purpose" (Romans 8:28, NASB).

> It has always been the experience of the children of God that when we walk daily in the will of God, even that which looks like tragedy and loss in the end will turn out to be blessing and gain.
>
> —*A. W. Tozer* [17]

In the movie Zorba The Greek, Anthony Quinn, Zorba, tells the young English visitor, "Life is trouble, only death is not." Although the movie is far from being a model of Christian living, this one phrase powerfully sums up the Christian pilgrimage. Our walk with Jesus is filled with trouble and challenges that are often magnified, because the world and Satan hate to see a person fully committed to their Savior. Consequently, we need to mature in faith so we can see how big our God is: far bigger than any trial we can possibly face, and far bigger than anything we can imagine. Then, as our eyes are opened to His majesty, we can worship Him in praise and thanksgiving regardless of our circumstances knowing He causes all things to work together for good to those who love Him.

YOU ARE TOO WONDERFUL
O Lord, You are too wonderful to me.

When I follow Your way,
You are the light in my eyes,
You are the glow on my face;
You give me peace,
You give me joy,
You give me love;
my spirit tastes the joy of being in Your eternal presence in heaven.

O Lord, my heart's desire is to do Your will,
to be the person You created me to be,
to fulfill Your purpose for my life,
to live in the house of the Lord forever.

O Lord, You are too wonderful to me.

## *Reflections and Questions*

Look beyond the storms of your daily life to see how Jesus is causing all things to work together for good. Identify these "things" as the Holy Spirit illuminates them to you.

## *Challenge for This Week*

In prayer, give praise and thanks to Him who is carrying you through, even though there is still some way to go.

---

### *Memory Verse*

And we know that in all things God works for the good of those who love him, who have been called according to his purpose.

Romans 8:28

---

## *Readings for Week 18: Things Work Together*

Day 1 (__/__/__) - Exodus 33:12-23

Key verse: *The LORD replied, "My Presence will go with you, and I will give you rest"* (v. 14).

How did the Lord speak to you today and how did you respond?

______________________________________________

______________________________________________

______________________________________________

______________________________________________

Day 2 (__/__/__) - Psalm 16:1-11

Key verse: *You have made known to me the path of life; you will fill me with joy in your presence, with eternal pleasures at your right hand* (v. 11).

How did the Lord speak to you today and how did you respond?

______________________________________________

______________________________________________

______________________________________________

______________________________________________

Day 3 (__/__/__) - Psalm 84:1-12
   Key verse: *Blessed are those whose strength is in you, who have set their hearts on pilgrimage* (v. 5).

How did the Lord speak to you today and how did you respond?

_______________________________________________________________

_______________________________________________________________

_______________________________________________________________

_______________________________________________________________


Day 4 (__/__/__) - Isaiah 40:25-31
   Key verse: *…; but those who hope in the LORD will renew their strength. They will soar on wings like eagles; they will run and not grow weary, they will walk and not be faint* (v. 31).

How did the Lord speak to you today and how did you respond?

_______________________________________________________________

_______________________________________________________________

_______________________________________________________________

_______________________________________________________________


Day 5 (__/__/__) - Habakkuk 3:17-19
   Key verse: *The Sovereign LORD is my strength; he makes my feet like the feet of a deer, he enables me to go on the heights* (v. 19a).

How did the Lord speak to you today and how did you respond?

_______________________________________________________________

_______________________________________________________________

_______________________________________________________________

_______________________________________________________________


Day 6 (__/__/__) - Philippians 3:12-4:1
   Key verse: *I press on toward the goal to win the prize for which God has called me heavenward in Christ Jesus* (v. 14).

How did the Lord speak to you today and how did you respond?

_______________________________________________________________

_______________________________________________________________

_______________________________________________________________

_______________________________________________________________

# PART III: HIS VICTORY

Jesus Christ our Savior reigns. His is the victory!

**His victory** is when the nature of Jesus has uncontested ownership of our hearts.
**His victory** is when we live to fulfill the purpose Jesus has placed in our hearts.
**His victory** is when we follow the way of Jesus rather than the way of the world.

**His victory** is when we live daily in His presence with the fruit of the Spirit evident in our lives.
**His victory** is when we live daily in His presence and His abundant grace.
**His victory** is when we live daily in His presence with gifts of the Spirit bringing glory to God in our lives.

By this we are witnesses of His love.

Amen.

But thanks be to God! He gives us the victory through our Lord Jesus Christ.

1 Corinthians 15:57

We can know the fruit of the Spirit, our gifts of the Spirit, and participate in the Great Commission to "go and make disciples" when we ourselves are His disciples: when His nature has gained the victory over our old natures (Matthew 28:19).

# Week 19: Christ's Victory

## Jesus Christ our Savior reigns. His is the victory!

As the Israelites left the desert to enter the Promised Land, so they entered a time of warfare that required complete reliance on God for victory. Also, as we leave the "desert of life," by choosing to allow Jesus to be Lord of our lives, we enter a time of warfare for our souls (mind, will, and emotions) where Satan wants to keep us captive to the ways of the world. "But thanks be to God! He gives us the victory through our Lord Jesus Christ" (1 Corinthians 15:57).

> Ultimately, as with Israel, the day dawns when there comes an end to the dismal old self-life of despair and discouragement. In an act of bold faith in God we decide to abandon ourselves and capitulate completely to Christ. …. Then in implicit, unquestioning obedience we step out to comply with His wishes.
>
> This is a titanic pivot point in any person's walk with God. This is the crossing of the Jordan. …. From then on there is no looking back. There is no returning to the weary old wilderness days of the wretched desert years.
>
> —*W. Phillip Keller* [18]

Ephesians 6:11 tells us to "put on the full armor of God so that you can take your stand against the devil's schemes." This passage goes on to describe all the pieces of the armor of God which, with one exception, are defensive and protective so that we can stand the assaults of Satan, the prince of this world, as he works against us through life situations and people. This one exception is "the sword of the Spirit, which is the word of God." That is to say, the forces of evil are always turned back as we strike with the Word of God and this confirms how essential it is for us to be in His Word so we can know and apply His Word in the days of battle.

THE LORD'S WARRIORS

Hallelujah, the Lord God Almighty reigns! His is the victory. We are His warriors.

In the clash of armies, the warrior must look to the Lord for guidance, for protection, for strength, for courage, for wisdom, for compassion, for rest, for healing, for recovery, for victory. So in our daily battles for the Lord, we must look to Him for these same things in our words and our deeds.

And as the battle rages, it is sometimes difficult to know if the Lord is there; sometimes it seems as if the forces that oppose us are too strong; sometimes it seems that those who are willing to fight for Him are too few; sometimes we wonder if it is worth going on.

But God is faithful. His victory is not by superior numbers. His protection is not by superior armor. His attack is not by superior weapons. The Lord's victory is His and His alone, made possible by His unfailing grace that can overcome all things.

## Reflections and Questions

Identify some of the "battles" that you still experience where you withhold parts of your life from our Savior Jesus Christ and so quench the fullness of His Spirit.

## *Challenge for This Week*

In prayerful submission to Jesus, ask Him to show you the true source of the struggles in your life and the true source of the power to overcome.

### *Memory Verse*

He holds victory in store for the upright, he is a shield to those whose walk is blameless, for he guards the course of the just and protects the way of his faithful ones.

Proverbs 2: 7-8

## *Readings for Week 19: Christ's Victory*

Day 1 (__/__/__) - Deuteronomy 20:1-4

Key verse: *"For the LORD your God is the one who goes with you to fight for you…to give you victory"* (v. 4).

How did the Lord speak to you today and how did you respond?

_______________________________________________

_______________________________________________

_______________________________________________

_______________________________________________

Day 2 (__/__/__) - Psalm 44:1-8

Key verse: *I do not trust in my bow, my sword does not bring me victory; but you give us victory …* (vv. 6–7a).

How did the Lord speak to you today and how did you respond?

_______________________________________________

_______________________________________________

_______________________________________________

_______________________________________________

Day 3 (__/__/__) - Psalm 118:1-29

Key verse: *Shouts of joy and victory resound in the tents of the righteous: "The LORD's right hand has done mighty things!"* (v. 15).

How did the Lord speak to you today and how did you respond?

_______________________________________________

_______________________________________________

_______________________________________________

_______________________________________________

Day 4 (__/__/__) - Proverbs 2:1-8
   Key verse: *He holds victory in store for the upright, he is a shield to those whose walk is blameless, …* (v. 7).

How did the Lord speak to you today and how did you respond?

_______________________________________________________

_______________________________________________________

_______________________________________________________

_______________________________________________________


Day 5 (__/__/__) - Romans 8:28-39
   Key verse: *No, in all these things we are more than conquerors through him who loved us* (v. 37).

How did the Lord speak to you today and how did you respond?

_______________________________________________________

_______________________________________________________

_______________________________________________________

_______________________________________________________


Day 6 (__/__/__) - 1 Corinthians 15:50-58
   Key verse: *But thanks be to God! He gives us the victory through our LORD Jesus Christ* (v. 57).

How did the Lord speak to you today and how did you respond?

_______________________________________________________

_______________________________________________________

_______________________________________________________

_______________________________________________________

# Week 20: Jesus Only



*His victory is when the nature of Jesus has uncontested ownership of our hearts.*

For Jesus to have uncontested ownership of our hearts, we have to get to the point of recognizing our utter depravity apart from Him. It is only then that we can fully embrace the lordship of Jesus in our hearts.

> Victory begins with the name of Jesus on your lips; but it will not be consummated until the nature of Jesus is in your heart. This rule applies to every facet of spiritual warfare. Indeed, Satan will be allowed to come against the area of your weakness until you realize God's only answer is to become Christlike. As you begin to appropriate not just the name of Jesus, but His nature as well, the adversary will withdraw. Satan will not continue to assault you if the circumstances he designed to destroy you are now working to perfect you!
>
> —*Francis Frangipane* [19]

The flight from Los Angeles to Boston required a change of planes in Indianapolis, but the onward flight was cancelled and after a four hour delay I was rebooked on another flight that went via Washington, causing an additional two hour delay. When I boarded this flight my sense of communion with the Holy Spirit was lost, with the fruit of the Spirit replaced by my own frustrations and I cried out in silent prayer, "Oh Lord, how I fail You!"

However, once the flight took off I persevered to quiet my soul by reading a book by Charles Spurgeon, but I had little enthusiasm for the content and no release of my frustrations. Then the air hostess asked to see the book and realizing from the title that I was a Christian she went to get the book she was carrying with her: The Three Battlegrounds by Francis Frangipane that I quote from above.

What a blessing this book was as I understood for the first time the nature of the spiritual battles in our minds. And, yes, it was also an answer to those few words of prayer as I admitted my failings to the Lord. This understanding helped me on the road to releasing all to Jesus.

LORD MOST HIGH

> Praise You, praise You, praise You, Lord Most High!
> You turn my pride into humility.
> You turn my deceit into purity.
>
> Praise You, praise You, praise You, Lord Most High!
> You turn my self-seeking into loving.
> You turn my self-keeping into giving.
>
> Praise You, praise You, praise You, Lord Most High!
> You turn my worry into peace.
> You turn my woe into joy.
>
> Praise You, praise You, praise You, Lord Most High!
> You turn my caution into action.
> You turn my weakness into boldness.
>
> Praise You, praise You, praise You, Lord Most High!

## *Reflections and Questions*

How badly do you want to know the fullness of Christ's love for you?

## *Challenge for This Week*

Get apart with the Lord and pour out your heart to him. Do not leave His presence until you have transacted this most important decision: "Yes, Lord, I surrender all to You."

---

### *Memory Verse*

Whoever claims to live in him must walk as Jesus did.

1 John 2:6

---

## *Readings for Week 20: Only Jesus*

Day 1 (__/__/__) - Psalm 32:1-11

Key verse: *Then I acknowledged my sin to you and did not cover up my iniquity. I said, "I will confess my transgressions to the LORD"—and you forgave the guilt of my sin* (v. 5).

How did the Lord speak to you today and how did you respond?

_______________________________________________________

_______________________________________________________

_______________________________________________________

_______________________________________________________

Day 2 (__/__/__) - Psalm 51:1-19

Key verse: *Surely I was sinful at birth, sinful from the time my mother conceived me* (v. 5).

How did the Lord speak to you today and how did you respond?

_______________________________________________________

_______________________________________________________

_______________________________________________________

_______________________________________________________

Day 3 (__/__/__) - Isaiah 6:1-7

Key verse: *"Woe to me!" I cried. "I am ruined! For I am a man of unclean lips, and I live among a people of unclean lips, and my eyes have seen the King, the LORD Almighty"* (v. 5).

How did the Lord speak to you today and how did you respond?

_______________________________________________________

_______________________________________________________

_______________________________________________________

_______________________________________________________

Day 4 (__/__/__) - Isaiah 64:1-12
Key verse: *All of us have become like one who is unclean, and all our righteous acts are like filthy rags; we all shrivel up like a leaf, and like the wind our sins sweep us away* (v. 6).

How did the Lord speak to you today and how did you respond?

_______________________________________________________________________

_______________________________________________________________________

_______________________________________________________________________

_______________________________________________________________________

Day 5 (__/__/__) - Romans 7:14-25
Key verse: *What a wretched man I am! Who will rescue me from this body of death?* (v. 24).

How did the Lord speak to you today and how did you respond?

_______________________________________________________________________

_______________________________________________________________________

_______________________________________________________________________

_______________________________________________________________________

Day 6 (__/__/__) - 1 John 1:1 - 2:6
Key verse: *If we claim to be without sin, we deceive ourselves and the truth is not in us* (v. 1:8).

How did the Lord speak to you today and how did you respond?

_______________________________________________________________________

_______________________________________________________________________

_______________________________________________________________________

_______________________________________________________________________

# Week 21: Our Purpose in Christ

*His victory is when we live to fulfill the purpose Jesus has placed in our hearts.*

God wants us to succeed, but on His righteous terms and not our worldly terms. Consequently, as we draw closer to Jesus, the desires of our hearts also draw closer to fulfillment.

David gives us confirmation of this in Psalm 20:4 where he writes: "May he give you the desires of your heart and make all your plans succeed."

> The whole thing is nothing extraordinary, nothing special. It has been just a simple surrender, a simple yes to Christ, allowing him to do as he wants. That is why the work is his work. I'm just a little pencil in his hand.
>
> *—Mother Teresa* [20]

It may be that you have received a calling from the Lord; it may be that you sense in your heart that the Lord wants you to be engaged in a particular ministry; it may be that you have a deep concern for a group of people who are suffering. Whatever the nature of your desire to serve the Lord, as you set out on your walk with Him it is very likely and very human that your focus is on accomplishing these desires for His kingdom and your fulfillment.

But as we proceed along the road of life with Jesus, it seems that He is not too interested in us doing what is in our hearts to do; rather, He keeps bringing us back to the present and looking to see how closely we are following Him or going our own way. This frequently leads us to become frustrated with God, and indeed many Christians turn aside at this time, not willing to yield to His gentle hands that are trying to mold us into His likeness. Yet if we are faithful we eventually learn that our Lord wants us to live each day for His glory: it is the journey that is important to Him, not the achievement of the goal.

THE PURPOSE OF LIFE
> To live each day,
> where God has placed me,
> for His glory.

But that is not the end to the story, because as we yield fully to Him the desires of our hearts do start to become a beautiful reality by His sovereign grace.

## Reflections and Questions

How have the desires of your heart changed as you draw closer to Jesus?

## Challenge for This Week

As you read the daily Bible passages and spend time with the Lord in prayer this week, ask Him to show you how His purpose for your life and the desires of your heart can be one. If you already know this oneness, pray that you are also one with His way and His timing.

## *Memory Verse*

I pray also that the eyes of your heart may be enlightened in order that you may know the hope to which he has called you, the riches of his glorious inheritance in the saints, and his incomparably great power for us who believe.

Ephesians 1:18-19a

## *Readings for Week 21: Our Purpose In Christ*

Day 1 (__/__/__) - Joshua 1:1-11

Key verse: *"Be strong and very courageous. Be careful to obey all the law my servant Moses gave you; do not turn from it to the right or to the left, that you may be successful wherever you go"* (v. 7).

How did the Lord speak to you today and how did you respond?

______________________________________________

______________________________________________

______________________________________________

______________________________________________

Day 2 (__/__/__) - 2 Samuel 22:26-37

Key verse: *"With your help I can advance against a troop; with my God I can scale a wall"* (v. 30).

How did the Lord speak to you today and how did you respond?

______________________________________________

______________________________________________

______________________________________________

______________________________________________

Day 3 (__/__/__) - Psalm 33:1-22

Key verse: *May your unfailing love rest upon us, O LORD, even as we put our hope in you* (v. 22).

How did the Lord speak to you today and how did you respond?

______________________________________________

______________________________________________

______________________________________________

______________________________________________

Day 4 (__/__/__) - John 17:20-26
Key verse: *[Jesus prayed,] "I have made you known to them, and will continue to make you known in order that the love you have for me may be in them and that I myself may be in them"* (v. 26).

How did the Lord speak to you today and how did you respond?

_________________________________________________________________

_________________________________________________________________

_________________________________________________________________

_________________________________________________________________

Day 5 (__/__/__) - Ephesians 1:15-23
Key verse: *I pray also that the eyes of your heart may be enlightened in order that you may know the hope to which he has called you, …* (v. 18a).

How did the Lord speak to you today and how did you respond?

_________________________________________________________________

_________________________________________________________________

_________________________________________________________________

_________________________________________________________________

Day 6 (__/__/__) - Colossians 2:6-12
Key verse: *and you have been given fullness in Christ, who is the head over every power and authority* (v. 10).

How did the Lord speak to you today and how did you respond?

_________________________________________________________________

_________________________________________________________________

_________________________________________________________________

_________________________________________________________________

# Week 22: The Way of Jesus

*His victory is when we follow the way of Jesus rather than the way of the world.*

Now that we are close to the promised victory, Satan, that great deceiver, will seek to turn us aside: "Your enemy the devil prowls around like a roaring lion looking for someone to devour" (1 Peter 5:8b).

The great deceiver's presence will not be obvious to us, because he is the master of deceit; rather he will sow seeds of doubt in our minds. One of these seeds is to show us that there are just too many people who follow the way of the world for us to try and continue to follow the way of Jesus Christ. However, God's victory is not found in great numbers but in great faithfulness.

> So throughout the entire New Testament a sharp line is drawn between the Church and the world. There is no middle ground. The Lord recognizes no good natured "agreeing to disagree" so that the followers of the Lamb may adopt the world's ways and travel along the world's path. The gulf between the true Christian and the world is as great as that which separated the rich man and Lazarus. And, furthermore, it is the same gulf, that is, it is the gulf that divides the world of the ransomed from the world of fallen men.
>
> *—A. W. Tozer* [21]

Diary entry February 20th 2003:

Today I completed writing 'The Battle' that I had started in December 2002. Sometimes the words of these prose come to me as if poured out from heaven; sometimes it takes many weeks or months to wrestle the truth from God's Word by the guidance of His Spirit. 'The Battle' is the latter kind, and, indeed, it seems the very act of writing it has been a reflection of a battle in the heavenlies against the forces of evil. For, as I rewrote the second part and completed it today with the scriptures inserted, the anguish I had felt all week disappeared even as if the forces of evil had been defeated by the very power of God.

THE BATTLE

I desire to do Your will, my Lord, even with all my heart and all my soul and all my mind and all my strength—and yet I so often fail.

Is it just my sinfulness, my Lord?

Or is it the sin of this world that also entices me from His way?

Or, again, does the power of the evil one also seek to destroy my walk with You?

Often it seems that it is not just one of these evils, but all three battling against Your will for my life.

However,

With you, my Lord, there is victory over sin.

He himself bore our sins in his body on the tree, so that we might die to sins and live for righteousness; by his wounds you have been healed (1 Peter 2:24).

With you, my Lord, there is victory over the world.

> "In this world you will have trouble. But take heart! I have overcome the world" (John 16:33b).

With you, my Lord, there is victory over the evil one.

> … take up the shield of faith, with which you can extinguish all the flaming arrows of the evil one (Ephesians 6:16b).

With you, my Lord, victory is assured!

## Reflections and Questions

Do you allow prevailing worldly attitudes to silence your witness for Jesus Christ at home, at work, in social activities, or even in church activities? Or do you allow the Holy Spirit to work in you so that you are "salt" and "light" in all situations?

## Challenge for This Week

As you read the Bible passages this week see how God's way to achieve victory is different to man's way. Also reflect on your journey with our Lord to see if you are trying to face your difficulties and struggles by your own strength and the world's ways, or if you are allowing the Spirit of Christ to work in your life and the situation for His glory.

---

### Memory Verse

Don't you know that friendship with the world is hatred toward God? Anyone who chooses to be a friend of the world becomes an enemy of God.

James 4:4b

---

## Readings for Week 22: The Way Of Jesus

Day 1 (__/__/__) - Numbers 13:26 to 14:9

Key verse: *If the* Lord *is pleased with us, he will lead us into that land, a land flowing with milk and honey, and will give it to us* (v. 14:8).

How did the Lord speak to you today and how did you respond?

Day 2 (__/__/__) - 1 Kings 18:16-39

Key verse: *Then Elijah said to them, "I am the only one of the LORD's prophets left, but Baal has four hundred and fifty prophets"* (v. 22).

How did the Lord speak to you today and how did you respond?

______________________________________________________________

______________________________________________________________

______________________________________________________________

______________________________________________________________

Day 3 (__/__/__) - 2 Chronicles 20:1-26

Key verse: *"This is what the LORD says to you: 'Do not be afraid or discouraged because of this vast army. For the battle is not yours, but God's'"* (v. 15b).

How did the Lord speak to you today and how did you respond?

______________________________________________________________

______________________________________________________________

______________________________________________________________

______________________________________________________________

Day 4 (__/__/__) - Ephesians 2:1-10

Key verse: *As for you, you were dead in your transgressions and sins, in which you used to live when you followed the ways of this world and of the ruler of the kingdom of the air, the spirit who is now at work in those who are disobedient* (vv. 1-2).

How did the Lord speak to you today and how did you respond?

______________________________________________________________

______________________________________________________________

______________________________________________________________

______________________________________________________________

Day 5 (__/__/__) - James 4:1-10
   Key verse: …, *don't you know that friendship with the world is hatred toward God? Anyone who chooses to be a friend of the world becomes an enemy of God* (v. 4b).

How did the Lord speak to you today and how did you respond?

_______________________________________________________________________________

_______________________________________________________________________________

_______________________________________________________________________________

_______________________________________________________________________________


Day 6 (__/__/__) - 1 John 2:15-17
   Key verse: *Do not love the world or anything in the world. If anyone loves the world, the love of the Father is not in him* (v. 15).

How did the Lord speak to you today and how did you respond?

_______________________________________________________________________________

_______________________________________________________________________________

_______________________________________________________________________________

_______________________________________________________________________________

# Week 23: Fruit of the Spirit



*His victory is when we live daily in His presence with the
fruit of the Spirit evident in our lives.*

When we are born again, the full measure of the Holy Spirit is immediately available to us. However, because our sinful nature is still controlling us, the Spirit of God has little room to influence our lives. Therefore, it is only when we "have crucified the sinful nature with its passions and desires" that "love, joy, peace, patience, kindness, goodness, faithfulness, gentleness and self-control" come to stay (see Galatians 5:22-24).

> Put in its simplest terms, the Bible tells us we need the Spirit to bring fruit into our lives because we cannot produce godliness apart from the Spirit. In our own selves we are filled with all kinds of self-centered and self-seeking desires which are opposed to God's will for our lives. In other words two things need to happen in our lives. First, the sin in our lives needs to be thrust out. Second, the Holy Spirit needs to come in and fill our lives, producing the fruit of the Spirit.
>
> —*Billy Graham* [22]

Summer in Abu Dhabi can be unbearable, with temperatures about 120° F and humidity close to 100 percent. Even if the conditions are moderated by a breeze coming off the desert, there is the possibility of a sand storm to add to the miserable climate.

I have been to the United Arab Emirates on many business trips, but this one was particularly arduous, requiring safety inspections of three massive drilling rigs that were under construction. Just to reach the drill floor of these rigs required climbing fourteen flights of stairs in the torrid conditions. The business meetings were also very intense, as there are many challenges to keeping a safe working environment in countries that do not have strict safety standards or consequences for workers being injured.

However, this trip was a wonderful blessing as the Lord was with me and sustained me by His love and the presence of the fruit of the Spirit. I truly could sing to the Lord!

I SING TO YOU, LORD!

> I sing to You, Lord. You give me:
> Love over Indifference,
> Joy over Misery,
> Peace over Turmoil.
>
> I sing to You, Lord. You give me:
> Patience over Irritability,
> Kindness over Malice,
> Goodness over Immorality.
>
> I sing to You, Lord. You give me:
> Faithfulness over Fearfulness,
> Gentleness over Harshness,
> Self-control over Unrestraint.

I sing to You, Lord. You give me:
the fruit of the Spirit over
the fruit of my sinful nature.

I sing to You, Lord!

## *Reflections and Questions*

The Lord did not give us His presence with the fruit of the Spirit only for our own benefit, but also and more importantly, that our lives may be a witness to draw others to Him. How have you seen this happen in your life? And where have you seen the remnants of your worldly nature cause people to be cynical toward the message of our Savior?

## *Challenge for This Week*

Think and pray about how you can now follow Jesus in every detail of your life so that you can be "the aroma of Christ among those who are being saved and those who are perishing" (2 Corinthians 2:15).

---

### *Memory Verse*

For we are to God the aroma of Christ among those who are being saved and those who are perishing.

2 Corinthians 2:15

---

## *Readings for Week 23: The Fruit of the Spirit*

Day 1 (__/__/__) - John 4:1-14 and 7:37-39

Key verse: *"Whoever believes in me, as the Scripture has said, streams of living water will flow from within him"* (v. 7:38).

How did the Lord speak to you today and how did you respond?

_______________________________________________

_______________________________________________

_______________________________________________

_______________________________________________

Day 2 (__/__/__) - Acts 2:14-41

Key verse: *Peter replied, "Repent and be baptized, every one of you, in the name of Jesus Christ for the forgiveness of your sins. And you will receive the gift of the Holy Spirit"* (v. 38).

How did the Lord speak to you today and how did you respond?

_______________________________________________

_______________________________________________

_______________________________________________

_______________________________________________

Day 3 (__/__/__) - Romans 8:1-17
   Key verse: *The mind of sinful man is death, but the mind controlled by the Spirit is life and peace; … (v. 6).*

How did the Lord speak to you today and how did you respond?

_______________________________________________

_______________________________________________

_______________________________________________

_______________________________________________

Day 4 (__/__/__) - 2 Corinthians 3:7-18
   Key verse: *And we, who with unveiled faces all reflect the LORD's glory, are being transformed into his likeness with ever-increasing glory, which comes from the LORD, who is the Spirit (v. 18).*

How did the Lord speak to you today and how did you respond?

_______________________________________________

_______________________________________________

_______________________________________________

_______________________________________________

Day 5 (__/__/__) - Ephesians 4:17-32
   Key verse: *And do not grieve the Holy Spirit of God, with whom you were sealed for the day of redemption (v. 30).*

How did the Lord speak to you today and how did you respond?

_______________________________________________

_______________________________________________

_______________________________________________

_______________________________________________

Day 6 (__/__/__) - 1 Thessalonians 5:12-24
   Key verse: *Do not put out the Spirit's fire; … (v. 19, NIV). Do not quench the Spirit (v. 19, NASB).*

How did the Lord speak to you today and how did you respond?

_______________________________________________

_______________________________________________

_______________________________________________

_______________________________________________

# Week 24: God's Grace

*His victory is when we live daily in His presence and in His abundant grace in our lives.*

It may seem that the fruit of the Spirit do not in themselves equip us too well for the rigors of daily living. However, these "fruit" are accompanied by the awesome grace of God working in the details of our lives as we allow Jesus to be Lord of all. Indeed, it is this awesome grace that God providentially works in the situations we face enabling His will to be done through us!

Paul summed this up in His letter to the Romans: "How much more will those who receive God's abundant provision of grace and of the gift of righteousness reign in life through the one man, Jesus Christ" (Romans 5:17b).

> He will give grace, but you must pray for it. He will give grace, but you must search the Scriptures to find it. He will give grace, but you must observe the means He has given. You must get in communion with God and draw near to Him. You must have your times of quiet retirement and still meditation, for although the Lord makes the pipe of His grace flow into the marketplace, yet He expects His people to bring their pitchers there to get them filled. … He will give grace, but we must go to Him for it in His own appointed way.
>
> *—Charles Spurgeon* [23]

In chapter twenty of 2 Chronicles there is a vivid description of a time in the reign of King Jehoshaphat when the Moabites and the Ammonites came with a vast army to war against Judah. The Israelites faced certain defeat, but the Lord promised to be with Jehoshaphat and as they set out to meet the invaders, Jehoshaphat stood and said, "Listen to me, Judah and people of Jerusalem! Have faith in the Lord your God and you will be upheld …." After consulting the people, Jehoshaphat appointed men to sing to the Lord and to praise him for the splendor of his holiness as they went out at the head of the army, saying: "Give thanks to the Lord, for his love endures forever."

As they began to sing and praise, the Lord set ambushes against the invaders and they were defeated.

This passage teaches us a powerful lesson. Even though a situation may appear hopeless, we are to praise the Lord and trust in Him because He is the omnipotent God who works miracles on our behalf. Therefore, we can live with the peace and joy of the Holy Spirit even as we face insurmountable trials, because His grace can be poured into any situation to fulfill His purpose and bring Him glory.

It was an occasion when I was facing a very difficult trial of being out of work with no doors opening to earn a living that I became fearful of the uncertainty that lay ahead. However, the Lord did not allow me to wallow in defeat; rather, He urged me in my spirit to sing praises to Him for the victory that was to come!

REJOICE, REJOICE, REJOICE!
>Rejoice, rejoice, rejoice in Jesus our Savior.
>Rejoice, rejoice, rejoice in Jesus our Lord.
>Though my heart faints within me,
>and Your way cannot be seen,
>I rejoice in Jesus my Savior,
>I rejoice in Jesus my Lord.
>It's not my strength that allows this,

but His grace that is poured from above, so
I rejoice in Jesus my Savior,
I rejoice in Jesus my Lord.

Rejoice, rejoice, rejoice in Jesus our Savior.
Rejoice, rejoice, rejoice in Jesus our Lord.

## *Reflections and Questions*

How have you seen the power of God's grace enter into the details of your life? Also, where do you still snuff out this presence of the Holy Spirit, preferring to do things in your own way and your own strength?

## *Challenge for This Week*

One reason we reject the fruit and the power of the Holy Spirit is that we cannot believe that God would impart such incredible blessings upon us. Therefore, as you read His Word this week, also pray for the full armor of God (see Ephesians 6:10-18) so you can stand your ground against Satan, the great deceiver, who will want to sow seeds of doubt in your mind for you to discount the blessings that Christ so dearly wants to give.

---

### *Memory Verse*

But he said to me, "My grace is sufficient for you, for my power is made perfect in weakness." Therefore I will boast all the more gladly about my weaknesses, so that Christ's power may rest on me.

2 Corinthians 12:9

---

## *Readings for Week 24: God's Grace*

Day 1 (__/__/__) - Psalm 139:1-24

Key verse: *Where can I go from your Spirit? Where can I flee from your presence?* (v. 7).

How did the Lord speak to you today and how did you respond?

________________________________________

________________________________________

________________________________________

________________________________________

Day 2 (__/__/__) - Romans 5:12-21

Key verse: *..., how much more will those who receive God's abundant provision of grace and of the gift of righteousness reign in life through the one man, Jesus Christ* (v. 17b).

How did the Lord speak to you today and how did you respond?

________________________________________

________________________________________

________________________________________

________________________________________

Day 3 (__/__/__) - 2 Corinthians 12:1-10

Key verse: *But he said to me, "My grace is sufficient for you, for my power is made perfect in weakness." Therefore, I will boast all the more gladly about my weaknesses, so that Christ's power may rest on me* (v. 9).

How did the Lord speak to you today and how did you respond?

________________________________________________________________

________________________________________________________________

________________________________________________________________

________________________________________________________________

Day 4 (__/__/__) - 2 Thessalonians 1:3-12

Key verse: *We pray this so that the name of our LORD Jesus may be glorified in you, and you in him, according to the grace of our God and the LORD Jesus Christ* (v. 12).

How did the Lord speak to you today and how did you respond?

________________________________________________________________

________________________________________________________________

________________________________________________________________

________________________________________________________________

Day 5 (__/__/__) - 1 Timothy 1:12-17

Key verse: *The grace of our LORD was poured out on me abundantly, along with the faith and love that are in Christ Jesus* (v. 14).

How did the Lord speak to you today and how did you respond?

________________________________________________________________

________________________________________________________________

________________________________________________________________

________________________________________________________________

Day 6 (__/__/__) - Hebrews 4:14 to 5:10

Key verse: *Let us then approach the throne of grace with confidence, so that we may receive mercy and find grace to help us in our time of need* (v. 16).

How did the Lord speak to you today and how did you respond?

________________________________________________________________

________________________________________________________________

________________________________________________________________

________________________________________________________________

# Week 25: Gifts of the Spirit

*His victory is when we live daily in His presence with gifts of the Spirit bringing glory to God in our lives.*

As we draw close to Jesus, so we gain an understanding of the gifts of the Spirit that God wonderfully brings into our hearts, making each one of us a special part of the body of Christ.

"There are different kinds of gifts, but the same Spirit…. Now to each one the manifestation of the Spirit is given for the common good" (see 1 Corinthians 12:4 and 7).

> When members of a church begin considering spiritual gifts, they sometimes run into difficulty by thinking that God gives them some thing—like an ingredient called administration. No, He doesn't give some thing; He gives Himself. The Gift is a Person. The Holy Spirit equips you with His administrative ability. So His administration begins to become your administration. What you observe when you see a spiritual gift exercised is a manifestation of the Holy Spirit—you see the Holy Spirit equipping and enabling an individual with His abilities and capabilities to accomplish God's work.
>
> *—Henry T. Blackaby and Claude V. King* [24]

As the stresses and strains of the day come upon us it is very easy to lose touch with the presence of the Holy Spirit and fall back into our old ways of thinking. To guard against this I take five minutes or so in the middle of the morning to refocus on the Lord: sometimes in silent prayer at my desk; sometimes picking up my Bible that I leave by my desk and reading a short passage of scripture; sometimes reviewing a daily devotional that I may have copied to my diary. On this particular day I spent just a few moments in prayer, hoping to lay aside a frustrating incident that had just occurred, and as I did so the Holy Spirit enlightened my mind with these words.

GREAT IS THE LORD!

    Great is the Lord and the presence of His Spirit so mighty—
bringing fruit of love, joy, peace, patience, kindness, goodness, faithfulness, gentleness and self-control to each believer;
bringing gifts in many forms, all distributed so that the church, the body of Christ, may be complete;
bringing the grace of God into our lives each moment of the day!

    And what does the Lord my God require of me to receive such bounty?
That I love Him:

love Him with all my heart,

love Him with all my soul,

love Him with all my mind, and

love Him with all my strength.

    Oh, how great is the Lord!

God gives us His fruit. God gives us His grace. God gives us His gifts. Surely we should rejoice always.

## Reflections and Questions

The gifts of the Spirit that are identified in Romans 12:6-8, 1 Corinthians 12:8-10, Ephesians 4:11, and 1 Peter 4:10-11 are summarized below. Identify, as best you can, those gifts that the Lord has given you. Also identify how you are able to use your gifts for the common good.

| | | |
|---|---|---|
| Apostleship* | Prophesy | Shepherding |
| Miraculous Powers | Faith | Giving |
| Showing Mercy | Knowledge | Tongues |
| Encouraging | Evangelism | Teaching |
| Healing | Serving | Leadership |
| Wisdom | Discernment | Interpreting Tongues |

* Note: apostleship here is taken to mean today's missionary gift.

## Challenge for This Week

As you read the Word of God this week, ask for a clearer understanding of the gifts that He is giving you to help build up the body of Christ. Also if you need additional help in understanding the gifts of the Spirit you will find an excellent description in Billy Graham's book, The Holy Spirit.

---

### Memory Verse

From him the whole body, joined and held together by every supporting ligament, grows and builds itself up in love, as each part does its work.

Ephesians 4:16

---

## Readings for Week 25: Gifts of the Spirit

Day 1 (__/__/__) - Romans 12:1-8
   Key verse: *We have different gifts, according to the grace given us* (v. 6a).

How did the Lord speak to you today and how did you respond?

_______________________________________________

_______________________________________________

_______________________________________________

_______________________________________________

Day 2 (__/__/__) - 1 Corinthians 12:1-11
   Key verse: *There are different kinds of gifts, but the same Spirit* (v. 4).

How did the Lord speak to you today and how did you respond?

_______________________________________________

_______________________________________________

_______________________________________________

_______________________________________________

Day 3 (__/__/__) - 1 Corinthians 12:12-31

Key verse: *For we were all baptized by one Spirit into one body… Now the body is not made up of one part but of many* (vv. 13a and 14).

How did the Lord speak to you today and how did you respond?

________________________________________________

________________________________________________

________________________________________________

________________________________________________

Day 4 (__/__/__) - Ephesians 4:1-16

Key verse: *From him the whole body, joined and held together by every supporting ligament, grows and builds itself up in love, as each part does its work* (v. 16).

How did the Lord speak to you today and how did you respond?

________________________________________________

________________________________________________

________________________________________________

________________________________________________

Day 5 (__/__/__) - Hebrews 2:1-4

Key verse: *God also testified to it by signs, wonders and various miracles, and gifts of the Holy Spirit distributed according to his will* (v. 4).

How did the Lord speak to you today and how did you respond?

________________________________________________

________________________________________________

________________________________________________

________________________________________________

Day 6 (__/__/__) - 1 Peter 4:1-11

Key verse: *Each one should use whatever gift he has received to serve others, faithfully administering God's grace in its various forms* (v. 10).

How did the Lord speak to you today and how did you respond?

________________________________________________

________________________________________________

________________________________________________

# *Week 26: Go and Make Disciples*

## *By this we witness His love.*

This study is about learning to follow Jesus, and just as Jesus said to His disciples two thousand years ago, "Come, follow me, and I will make you fishers of men," so He says the same thing to us today (Mark 1:17).

> Here finally is where we must all evaluate the contribution that our life and witness is making to the supreme purpose of him who is the Savior of the world. Are those who have followed us to Christ now leading others to him and teaching them to make disciples like ourselves? Note, it is not enough to rescue the perishing, though this is imperative; nor is it sufficient to build up newborn babes in the faith of Christ, although this too is necessary if the first fruit is to endure; in fact, it is not sufficient just to get them out winning souls, as commendable as this work may be. What really counts in the ultimate perpetuation of our work is the faithfulness with which our converts go out and make leaders out of their converts, not simply more followers.
>
> —*Robert E. Coleman* [25]

In this study guide I have shared some of the marker stones in my pilgrimage with Jesus, and what an incredible journey that has been and continues to be. Our Savior is also calling you to an incredible journey. Will you follow Him?

WHAT A PILGRIMAGE!
What a pilgrimage with Jesus by our side!
What a pilgrimage with the spirit of self replaced with the Spirit of God!
What a pilgrimage knowing the presence of the living God!

A pilgrimage that starts by being washed by the blood of the Lamb so that we can come openly before the throne of grace!
A pilgrimage that continues by being transformed by the renewing of our minds knowing the awesome presence of God the Father, God the Son and God the Holy Spirit!
A pilgrimage that forms a journey of life for His glory!

## *Reflections and Questions*

Is your life a constant witness of our Savior in word, in deed, and in attitude —to your family, to your friends, to your neighbors, to your work associates, and to others you meet each day?

Few will be able to give an honest *yes* answer to this question; however, identify how you have been able to become more of an "aroma of Christ among those who are being saved and those who are perishing" as you have participated in this study (2 Corinthians 2:15).

## *Challenge for This Week*

As Jesus gains the victory in our lives, He also calls us to go and to make disciples so that His victory may be multiplied.

## Memory Verse

Therefore go and make disciples of all nations, baptizing them in the name of the Father and of the Son and of the Holy Spirit, and teaching them to obey everything I have commanded you. And surely I am with you always, to the very end of the age.

Matthew 28:19-20

## Readings for Week 26: Go and Make Disciples

Day 1 (__/__/__) - Matthew 5:13-16

Key verse: *"In the same way, let your light shine before men, …"* (v. 16a).

How did the Lord speak to you today and how did you respond?

_______________________________________________

_______________________________________________

_______________________________________________

_______________________________________________

Day 2 (__/__/__) - 2 Corinthians 2:12 to 3:6

Key verse: *For we are to God the aroma of Christ among those who are being saved and those who are perishing* (v. 2:15).

How did the Lord speak to you today and how did you respond?

_______________________________________________

_______________________________________________

_______________________________________________

_______________________________________________

Day 3 (__/__/__) - 2 Corinthians 4:1-18

Key verse: *It is written: "I believed; therefore I have spoken." With that same spirit of faith we also believe and therefore speak …* (v. 13).

How did the Lord speak to you today and how did you respond?

_______________________________________________

_______________________________________________

_______________________________________________

_______________________________________________

Day 4 (__/__/__) - 2 Corinthians 5:11 to 6:2

Key verse: *We are therefore Christ's ambassadors, as though God were making his appeal through us* (v. 5:20a).

How did the Lord speak to you today and how did you respond?

_______________________________________________________________________________

_______________________________________________________________________________

_______________________________________________________________________________

_______________________________________________________________________________

Day 5 (__/__/__) - Philippians 2:12-18

Key verse: ..., *so that you may become blameless and pure, children of God without fault in a crooked and depraved generation, in which you shine like stars in the universe as you hold out the word of life* ... (vv.15-16a).

How did the Lord speak to you today and how did you respond?

_______________________________________________________________________________

_______________________________________________________________________________

_______________________________________________________________________________

_______________________________________________________________________________

Day 6 (__/__/__) - 2 Timothy 3:10 to 4:8

Key verse: *Preach the Word; be prepared in season and out of season; correct, rebuke and encourage—with great patience and careful instruction* (v. 4:2).

How did the Lord speak to you today and how did you respond?

_______________________________________________________________________________

_______________________________________________________________________________

_______________________________________________________________________________

_______________________________________________________________________________

# *Conclusion*

Paul's charge to Timothy provides a fitting conclusion to *Following Jesus in the Details of Life* by giving us the example of Paul walking with Jesus in the details of life and so fulfilling the Great Commission to "go and make disciples."

You, however, know all about my teaching, my way of life, my purpose, faith, patience, love, endurance, persecutions, sufferings—what kinds of things happened to me in Antioch, Iconium and Lystra, the persecutions I endured. Yet the Lord rescued me from all of them. In fact, everyone who wants to live a godly life in Christ Jesus will be persecuted, while evil men and imposters will go from bad to worse, deceiving and being deceived. But as for you, continue in what you have learned and become convinced of, because you know those from whom you learned it, and how from infancy you have known the holy Scriptures, which are able to make you wise for salvation through faith in Christ Jesus. All Scripture is God-breathed and is useful for teaching, rebuking, correcting and training in righteousness, so that the man of God may be thoroughly equipped for every good work.

In the presence of God and of Christ Jesus, who will judge the living and the dead, and in view of his appearing and his kingdom, I give you this charge: Preach the Word; be prepared in season and out of season; correct, rebuke and encourage—with great patience and careful instruction. For the time will come when men will not put up with sound doctrine. Instead, to suit their own desires, they will gather around them a great number of teachers to say what their itching ears want to hear. They will turn their ears away from the truth and turn aside to myths. But you, keep your head in all situations, endure hardship, do the work of an evangelist, discharge all the duties of your ministry.

For I am already being poured out like a drink offering, and the time has come for my departure. I have fought the good fight, I have finished the race, I have kept the faith. Now there is in store for me the crown of righteousness, which the Lord, the righteous Judge, will award to me on that day—and not only to me, but also to all who have longed for his appearing.

2 Timothy 3:10 to 4:8

# *Endnotes*



1. Andrew Murray, *Let Us Draw Nigh* (Fort Washington, PA: Christian Literature Crusade, 1974).

2. John R. W. Stott, *Baptism and Fullness* (Downers Grove IL: InterVarsity Press, 1975).

3. Mother Teresa, *My Life for the Poor* (New York, NY: Ballantine Books, 1987).

4. Dietrich Bonhoeffer, *The Cost of Discipleship* (New York, NY: Macmillan Publishing Co., 1949).

5. Martin Luther, *Sermons of Martin Luther* (Grand Rapids, MI: Baker Book House, 1989, vol. 2).

6. Oswald Chambers, *My Utmost For His Highest* (Grand Rapids, MI: Discovery House, 1992).

7. Billy Graham, *Storm Warning* (Dallas TX: Word Publishing, 1992).

8. Martin Luther, *Sermons of Martin Luther* (Grand Rapids, MI: Baker Book House, 1989, vol. 5).

9. Andrew Murray, *The Believer's Prayer Life* (Minneapolis, MN: Bethany House Publishers, 1983).

10. C. S. Lewis, *Mere Christianity* (New York, NY: Macmillan Publishing Company, 1943).

11. Jack W. Hayford, *The Power and the Blessing* (Wheaton, IL: Victor Books, 1994).

12. Doug Sherman and William Hendricks, *Your Work Matters to God* (Colorado Springs, CO: Navpress, 1987).

13. Patrick M. Morley, *Walking with Christ in the Details of Life* (Nashville, TN: Thomas Nelson Publishers, 1992).

14. Max Lucado, *Six Hours One Friday* (Portland, OR: Multnomah, 1989).

15. John R. W. Stott, *The Cross Of Christ* (Downers Grove, IL: InterVarsity Press, 1986).

16. Charles Spurgeon, *Spiritual Warfare in a Believer's Life* (Lynnwood, WA: Emerald Books, 1993).

17. A. W. Tozer, *Christ The Eternal Son* (Camp Hill, PA: Christian Publications, 1991).

18. W. Phillip Keller, *Joshua: Man of Fearless Faith* (Waco, TX: Word Books, 1983).

19. Francis Frangipane, *The Three Battlegrounds* (Cedar Rapids, IA: Arrow Publications, 1989).

20. Mother Teresa, *Total Surrender* (Ann Arbor, MI: Servant Publications, 1985).

21. A. W. Tozer, *The Divine Conquest* (Uhrichsville, OH: Barbour and Company, Inc., 1950).

22. Billy Graham, *The Holy Spirit* (Dallas TX: Word Publishing, 1978).

23. Charles Spurgeon, *Grace Abounding in a Believer's Life* (Lynnwood, WA: Emerald Books, 1994).

24. Henry T. Blackaby and Claude V. King, *Experiencing God* (Nashville. TN: LifeWay Press, 1990).

25. Robert E. Coleman, *The Master Plan of Evangelism* (Grand Rapids, MI: Fleming H. Revell, 1972).

# Companion Book

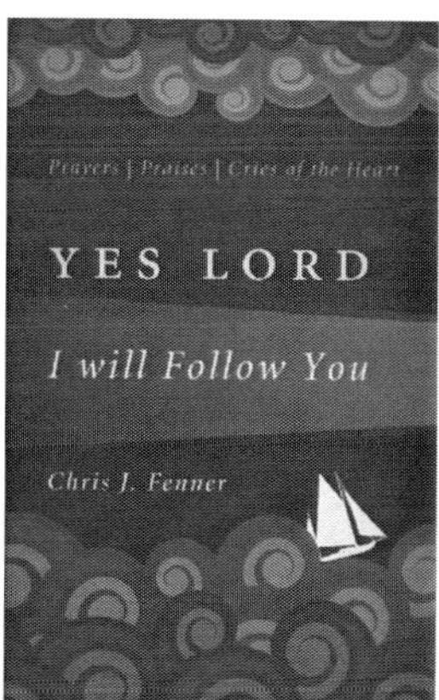

Today we need a great revival in America. As in the time of Elijah, we need the one and only true God to make Himself known.

In *Yes, Lord, I Will Follow You*, Chris Fenner documents his spiritual pilgrimage in prayers, praises and cries of his heart joining the ancient Israelites in declaring: "The Lord—he is God! The Lord—he is God!" He invites you to join him.

ISBN 978-1-61862-348-5

Pick up a copy today at
www.tatepublishing.com
TATE PUBLISHING, Mustang OK

# Prayer Companion

*Prayers of the Bible for Today* is a simple but beautiful compilation of the prayers of Scripture the conversations between ordinary people and their God-organized to facilitate study and meditation. Take time to read how, since the beginning of time, man has cried out to his Creator for solace, direction, healing, forgiveness and relationship, and see how Yahweh has lovingly answered. This is a wonderful way to understand more deeply how much we need to communicate with our Lord and God.

ISBN 978-0-9815-4190-7

Pick up a copy today at www.hisvp.com
HIS VICTORY PUBLISHING, Katy TX